Psalm 23

Discovery House Publishers

Books, music, and videos that feed the soul with the Word of God

Box 3566 Grand Rapids, MI 49501

The Song of a Passionate Heart

Psalm 23

Hope & Rest from the Shepherd

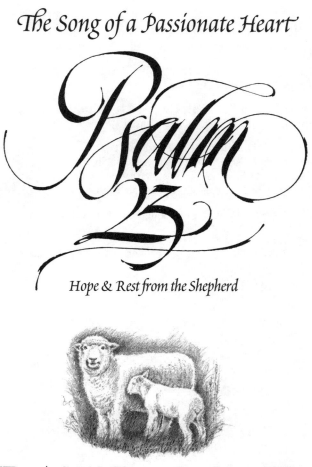

DAVID ROPER

Psalm 23: The Song of a Passionate Heart
© 1994 by David Roper. All rights reserved.

Discovery House Publishers is affiliated with RBC Ministries,
Grand Rapids, Michigan 49512

Discovery House books are distributed to the trade exclusively
by Barbour Publishing, Inc., Uhrichsville, Ohio 44683

Library of Congress Cataloging-in-Publication Data

Roper, David, 1933–
      Psalm 23 : the song of a passionate heart : hope and rest
from the shepherd /
    David Roper.
        p.   cm.
    ISBN 0-929239-86-5
    1. Bible. O.T. Psalm XXIII—Meditations. I. Title
BS1450 23rd.R66   1994
223'.206—dc20   94-9196
                                                        CIP

Printed in the United States of America

01 03 04 02 00
CHG
9 10 12 13 11 8

CONTENTS

DEDICATION

In fond memory of my mentor and dear friend

Ray Stedman

Who never sold the truth to serve the hour,
Nor haggled with eternal God for power.

THE SLOPE THROUGH DARKNESS

The great world's altar stairs,
That slope through darkness up to God.

—ALFRED TENNYSON

I CAME HOME FROM WORK ONE EVENING a few years ago and realized that I had gone flat. Just a blue Monday, I thought, or a bad case of the blahs. Surely a good night's sleep would set things right. But I was wrong.

During the days that followed I descended into a very dark place. I woke up morning after morning in the grip of melancholy, struggling to pull myself out of my gloom. I felt as if I were clinging to the side of a bottomless pit, my hand-holds precarious, afraid to move for fear I would plunge into a dark abyss.

Work became painful duty, a desperate effort. People with problems were a bother; friends with sunny, cheerful dispositions were a special trial. I wanted to get away from everything and every-one—take early retirement, build a cabin in the woods, or get a permanent job in a lighthouse. I cared for nothing. I enjoyed nothing. I had nothing to live for, and I could think of nothing for which I was willing to die.

Oh, there were flashes of delight—occasions that led me to think that I might be out of the dol-drums, but then I would slip again into the old groove of my misery. Each time I moved closer to despair. I could deal with the dreariness; it was the hope that was hardest to bear.

Friends suggested that my joyless state was the result of stresses, losses, or that I was getting a little long in the tooth—but so what? What could I do? I sought good counsel. I read good books. But like Al Capp's Joe Bfstx, I couldn't get out from under my cloud. Nothing displaced the darkness. Every day was a new shade of blue.

Then one morning something triggered the memory of an old poem—the Twenty-third Psalm—and the lyrics of that work became my safety line. I awakened morning by morning and seized on its words. I stuck to them like a limpet, reciting the words, reflecting on them, proclaiming them to myself. The Twenty-third Psalm became my creed.

One spring morning, not long ago, I woke up; the clouds had dispersed and the sun was beginning to shine. I don't know what brought me out of the darkness, but one thing I do know: My melancholy wasn't wasted. It was part of the good that God had determined to do for me. In the end, I could begin to say with Job, "My ears had heard of you but now my eyes have seen you" (Job 42:5).

What follows are some of the glimpses of God that came my way—a stream of thoughts emanating from the journal I kept during my Dark Age and my subsequent memories and musings. I share them with you in the hope that they will lead you to take another look at this old poem and at that Great Shepherd of the Sheep—the only good shepherd worthy of the name.

A PSALM OF DAVID

MICHELANGELO'S MARBLE STATUE OF DAVID stands
today in the Galleria dell' Accademia in Florence,
Italy—eighteen feet tall.

Michelangelo was right to sculpt David with
such immensity: He was a giant of a man, combining

in himself the military genius of Alexander the Great, the political savvy of Abraham Lincoln, the musical talent of Beethoven, the literary skill of Shakespeare, the hand-eye coordination of Joe Montana.

But the real measure of David's magnitude was his obsession with God: "One thing I ask of the LORD," he wrote. "This is what I seek: that I may dwell in the house of the LORD all the days of my life, to gaze upon the beauty of the LORD and to seek him in his temple" (Psalm 27:4). He was a man who was preoccupied with the love of God.

Yet, there was that other obsession: David was often consumed by pride, ambition, and lust. Capable of any sin and culpable of many, he frequently gave in to sudden, careless passion and that more deadly device—deliberate and determined evil.

That was David—eaten by lust and by the love of God. His dual obsessions make him familiar to me. He's my kind of man! More importantly, he was God's kind of man as well: "A man after his own heart" is the way God put it (1 Samuel 13:14). Ah, the fools God chooses!

Michelangelo took almost four years to finish his statue of David. The task was difficult because he was working with a piece of flawed marble. The block had been damaged when it was removed from the quarry.

So it was with David. He was flawed in his origins, abused as a child, left all alone, and nearly ruined. The world never met his needs.

But God did. He saw that lonely, ragged, love-starved boy as no one else did and set out to shape him into the man He envisioned David to be. It was hard work because David was deeply flawed, but God never gave up until the deed was done. Out of that labor, David's Twenty-third Psalm was born.

Some say the psalm was one of David's first efforts, composed while he was still a youth. But I disagree. Though the poem enshrines the memories and metaphors of David's early years, it is the thoughts of someone nearer the end of life than the beginning. Only a mature mind can sort out the complexities of life and fix on the things that matter. Only an old soul knows that very few things are necessary—actually only one.

"WANTING"

Most of the time,
I'm half-way content.

—BOB DYLAN

IN THE MOTION PICTURE *CITY SLICKERS*, three New York men head for the Old West hoping to find that one thing that satisfies.

The main character is Mitch Robbins, a wise-cracking, thirty-nine-year-old advertising salesman who had "lost his smile." Mitch had a lot going for

9

him—a charming wife, two handsome children, a spacious apartment on Roosevelt Island, two good buddies, and a quirky sense of humor. But the joy had gone out of his life. His birthdays, which used to bring him such happiness, now filled him only with sadness, each one reminding him that he still had not found out what life was for.

Mitch's two friends, Ed and Phil, shared his malaise and dreamed up the idea of joining a cattle drive from New Mexico to Colorado. (The year before they had run with the bulls in Pamplona, Spain.) The Old West seemed just the right place to shake off their unhappiness.

When the three men got to the ranch they were greeted by the last of the Marlboro Men, a leathery old cowboy named Curly, whom Robbins characterized as "a saddle bag with eyes." Under Curly's stern tutoring, Robbins and his friends learned to ride and rope before joining the sweaty brotherhood of drovers.

In Robbins' eyes, Curly was a kind of elemental male—a gruff, earthy man who rarely spoke, wore a perpetual smile, and was fearless, invulnerable, and all-knowing. While trailing the herd, Robbins asked Curly the secret of his assurance.

Curly replied, "You've got to find that one thing."

The trouble was, Mitch had no idea what that one thing was and Curly wasn't talking. Then the old buckaroo died before anyone could uncover the secret of his poise.

The moral of the movie, if there is one, is that each of us must find the "one thing" that will turn us into satisfied, self-assured versions of ourselves. The only problem is, when the house lights go up we're still in the dark: We have no idea what that one thing is.

That elusive "one thing"

Something keeps calling to us: something familiar and yet far away, something we cannot name. It fills us with a vague sense of discontent, a "wanting" for something we cannot identify. "You don't know what it is you want," mused Mark Twain, "but it just fairly makes your heart ache, you want it so much."

The wanting draws us on, promising us that satisfaction and happiness lie just ahead, filling us with restlessness, and keeping us on the move. Yet when we arrive we cannot rest. That's why we enjoy the quest, but not the conquest; the hunt, but not the kill; and that's why finishing can be almost unbearable.

Blaise Pascal, a seventeenth-century philosopher, had this to say:

> When I have set myself now and then to consider the various distractions of men, the toils and dangers to which they expose themselves in the court or in the camp, whence arise so many quarrels and passions, such daring and often such evil exploits, etc., I have discovered that all these misfortunes of men arise from one thing only, that they are unable to stay quietly in their own chamber. . . . Hence it comes that play, the society of women, war and offices of State are sought after. . . . Hence it comes that men so love noise and movement.

I'm always in a hurry to get things done;
I rush and rush until life's no fun.
All I really gotta do is live and die,
but I'm in a hurry and I don't know why.

—ALABAMA

The world intensifies our restlessness. Advertisements entice us to buy this, spend that, and to borrow against tomorrow so we can have what we want today. Generous incentives, rebates, markdowns, sales packages, and good deals urge us on, creating desires that we never knew we had.

The more we have, the more we want. Like a child who has opened a dozen gifts, we think more about what we didn't get than about what we did.

"Is this all there is?" we ask. "Isn't there something more?" It's not that we're greedy; it's just that something has been promised that we've not yet received.

Sex is not the solution, no matter what we're told.

You may recall Mr. Natural, Robert Crum's combination guru and dirty old man whose social comments enlivened the pages of campus newspapers in the 1960s. In one segment Mr. Natural and his student sidekick watch a miniskirted woman walk by. "Is sex the answer, Mr. Natural?" asks the young man. "No, my boy," Mr. Natural replies, "Sex is the question."

Indeed it is. Despite the information glut and all the propaganda in its favor, sex remains a great mystery. Our relentless pursuit of happiness through "good sex" verifies the Rolling Stones' old maxim: "I can't get no satisfaction." What sensual enjoyment remains is little more than a momentary refuge from misery.

It's ironic: the act which, more than any other, ought to assuage loneliness only intensifies it. Where is this great sex that is everywhere advertised but nowhere delivered? Where is the romance and intimacy for which we long? Tina Turner belts out her poignant creed: "What's love got to do with it?" Eventually we too learn to get along without the complications of love.

Friendships don't satisfy. At least they don't touch the deeper currents of life and love for which we long. "Even with the loved around me, still my heart says I am lonely," sighs some forgotten poet. Where is the human tenderness we seek—the readiness to love and accept? When we ask our friends to take away our loneliness we force on them a burden too heavy for anyone to bear. They let us down or go away and we go looking for someone else to curse with our demands. We are very difficult people. All we want is boundless love.

Parents never come through—especially fathers. For some the term *father* brings only blighted memories. To them it means all they've longed for and missed out on in life. Even those of us who had good fathers often felt they weren't what we wanted or needed them to be. We grew up trying to win their approval yet never receiving the validation we sought. "There is never enough father," Robert Bly laments.

As I stood beside my father's casket a few years ago, my wife, Carolyn, speaking in her quiet wisdom, said to me, "It's too late, isn't it?"

Exactly. Too late to gain his approval. A line from one of Len Deighton's books came to mind: "Do we never shed the tyranny of our father's love?"

Education yields only fragmentary results. We do time in various institutions, taking soundings here and there, but we never get to the bottom of things. There's so much labor in learning, so much to know that we cannot know. "I tasted wisdom," said one philosopher, "but it was far from me." That's the silent conclusion of everyone who matriculates. Perhaps that's why there's so much melancholy on campuses.

> *Myself when young did eagerly frequent*
> *Doctor and saint and heard great argument*
> *About it and about, but evermore*
> *Came out by the same door wherein I went.*
>
> —OMAR KHAYYAM

Success is never final. The long climb from the bottom to the top is exhilarating. We play all the petty games. We endure the privation, the competition, the demands, the drudgery, the long commutes. There's always one more deal to make, one more sale to push through, one more rung to climb, one more achievement to reach before we'll feel OK. We put in the time, we pay the price, and if we're lucky one transaction puts us over the top. But what then? The top is never the pinnacle we thought it would be.

Success is counted sweetest by those who ne'er succeed.

—**EMILY DICKINSON**

In an interview with Barbara Walters, Ted Turner confessed that "success is an empty bag." Money talks, but mostly it lies. It deceives us into believing that good fortune will bring satisfaction and security. But having enough is never enough. Having more is the goad that drives us. We pity the disillusioned, lonely, old tycoon with his money fixation, but we don't learn the lesson: "Whoever loves money never has money enough; whoever loves wealth is never satisfied with his income" (Ecclesiastes 5:10).

"Fame is fleeting" may be among the truest words ever spoken. We may do something or say something that turns heads and causes people to stare at us for a few days, but soon we're forgotten. Emerson was right, "Every hero becomes a bore at last." (And there's nothing quite so heartrending as a has-been trying to make a comeback.)

Marriage is not what it's cracked up to be. Despite the assurance of countless fairy tales, there's no direct relationship between getting married and living happily forever after. Couples start out well but fail because the emptiness and the ache of loneliness are so deep no one can touch them. And then for some desperate souls there are affairs (to use the lighthearted term that we apply to such disastrous ordeals), and then the crude finalities: divorces, bitter custody fights, the demolition of once-happy families, and the estrangement of little ones who are left behind.

Children are a delight. They offer us great happiness but also cause us terribly hard work and at times great suffering.

And then they leave home, as they should, and for some parents the empty nest is more than they can endure. Children are not the final achievement that we seek.

For many, retirement is the chief end. They spend all their adult years trying to make enough money to retire. Then, having reached their goal, they find it empty. Thoreau called it "destination sickness." There they are: exhausted from years of playing the game, well aware that time is running out. All the years spent worrying, scheming, and maneuvering are now meaningless. We see retirees everywhere with that dead look in their eyes. Having "arrived" they find nothing left for which to live.

> Since I have retired from life's competition
>> Each day is filled with complete repetition.
> I get up each morning and dust off my wits,
>> Go pick up the paper and read the obits.
>
> If my name isn't there, I know I'm not dead,
>> I get a good breakfast and go back to bed.
>> —UNKNOWN

Then there is old age, with its failing pride and fading power—and regret. We're "hung by our history," as they say. We look back and see the past strewn with the debris of our sin. Yet there's nothing we can do about it. All history, including our own, is unrepeatable.

Let me disclose the gifts reserved for age
To set a crown upon your lifetime's effort.
First, the cold friction of expiring sense
Without enchantment, offering no promise
But bitter tastelessness of shadow fruit
As body and soul begin to fall asunder.
Second, the conscious impotence of rage
At human folly, and the laceration
Of laughter at what ceases to amuse.
And last the rending pain of reenactment
Of all that you have done, and been; the shame
of motives late revealed, and the awareness
Of things ill done and done to others' harm
Which once you took for virtue.
The fools' approval stings and honour stains.

—T. S. ELIOT

And finally, there is the Big Chill. "Time is no healer," as some have said. "The patient dies." Death stalks us relentlessly. There's no escape. "The statistics are very impressive," George Bernard Shaw grumbled, "One out of every one person dies."

It boggles the mind to think of all the money, time, and energy we spend trying to stave off death —the medical profession, the defense budget, the cosmetics industry. But despite all the schemes we devise to stay alive, or at least look alive as long as possible, we only delay the inevitable. Ashes to ashes; dust to dust. Everybody, no matter how enduring, descends to decay and there's nothing anyone can do about it.

> Like a hen before a cobra, we find ourselves incapable of doing anything at all in the presence of the very thing that seems to call for the most drastic and decisive action. The disquieting thought, that stares at us like a face with a freezing grin, is that there is, in fact, nothing we can do. Say what we will, dance how we will, we will soon enough be a heap of ruined feathers and bones, indistinguishable from the rest of the ruins that lie about. It will not appear to matter in the slightest whether we met the enemy with equanimity, shrieks, or a trumped-up gaiety, there we will be.
>
> —TOM HOWARD

In our fear of dying we try to trivialize it, shrink it, cut it down to size, but let's not kid ourselves: dying matters. Human emotions are governed by stock reactions, and the stock reaction to death is bitter: Why do we have to leave everything behind that we've worked for, made, and loved? It's appalling to think that the world will go on without us as though we had never been born.

That's why most of life is one long effort not to think about dying, but it does no good. Just about the time we've forgotten about it, some friend or acquaintance goes and we have to attend the funeral. The thought of our own death confronts us again, and we know that we too will end up under the ground. Suddenly life seems utterly senseless. "Why go on," we say "when every beat of our heart, like a muffled drum, is marching us closer to the grave?"

"Imagine," Blaise Pascal wrote, "a number of prisoners under sentence of death; if some of them were executed every day in the sight of others, the remainder would behold their fate in that of their companions and look at one another with anguish and despair, expecting their turn to come." This, he concludes, "represents the condition of mankind." Like the monks who stared at the skulls in their cells, we behold our own fate: *Summus Moribundus* (We are destined to die).

This is our condition, and this is our frustration—the frustration of our greatest "want" of all—to live forever. We want to achieve immortality, but dying is what we do. "Where will it all end, Mr. Natural?" "In the grave, my boy," the old sage replies. "In the grave."

Oh, to be sure, there are those who imagine themselves to be happy by not thinking about the futility of life nor the certainty of death and who try to suppress their disquietude by going for all the gusto. But pleasure only shelves our dissatisfaction; it doesn't remove it. When the fun's over it's over, and the old questions return: What's it all about? Why should we eat, drink, work, play, raise money and children, and fight a never-ending sequence of frustrations. What happiness can there be in a world where everyone is born to die? Where has all the hustling, striving, lusting, and spending brought us? Why do we feel so empty and guilty and sad?

> *Faces along the bar*
> *Cling to their average day.*
> *The lights must never go out,*
> *The music must always play*
> *Lest we know where we are,*
> *Lost in a haunted wood,*
> *Children afraid of the dark*
> *Who have never been happy or good.*
>
> —W. H. AUDEN

And so it comes to this: There is no earthly satisfaction. Marriage, family, achievement, money, celebrity, enlightenment, travel, collections, artistic creation, flamboyance, excess—nothing completes our joy. There is always that elusive something more. No lesson is more comprehensively taught in this world.

Oh, there are serendipitous occasions along the way—capricious moments when we experience pure delight—but those moments are fleeting, and we can neither capture the sensation nor repeat it. The feeling is gone and we just can't get it back.

> *Enjoyed no sooner but despised straight,*
> *Past reason hunted, and no sooner had*
> *Past reason hated as a swallowed bait*
> *On purpose laid to make the taker mad;*
> *Mad in pursuit and in possession so;*
> *Had, having, and in quest to have, extreme;*
> *A bliss in proof, and proved a very woe,*
> *Before, a joy proposed; behind a dream.*
>
> *All this world knows; yet none knows well*
> *To shun the heaven that leads men to this hell.*
>
> —WILLIAM SHAKESPEARE

It is indeed strange that we go on "mad in pursuit," making the same mistake every day, trust-

23

ing that life will someday reveal its long-concealed and exquisite plan, even though experience has taught us that no matter what we achieve or acquire, it does not contain the contentment we seek.

Why do we keep on seeking?

Simply put: because we *have* to. Our seeking is a stirring of absolute need, one that must be satisfied—our eternal need for God. Every desire, every aspiration, every hunger and thirst, every longing of our nature is nothing less than desire for God. As G. K. Chesterton said, even when men knock on the door of a brothel they are looking for God. We were born for His love and we cannot live without it. He is that "one thing" for which we have been looking all our lives. All that we desire is there, and infinitely more.

> *Ah, fondest, blindest, weakest;*
> *I am He whom thou seekest.*
>
> —FRANCIS THOMPSON

It may surprise you to know that your desire is nothing more than desire for God, especially those of you who may not be accustomed to church. But there are moments when you know it's true—when something awakens within you, "a longing on Saturday for something that would have repelled me on Sunday," as a friend of mine once said. Once aroused, that longing is never stilled.

We should listen to our wants. They are meant to draw us to the place where we shall never want. What stupendous simplicity: "The LORD is my shepherd; I shall not be in want."

> When God first made man,
> Having a glass of blessings standing by,
> "Let us" (said he) "pour on him all we can;
> Let the world's riches, which dispersed lie,
>   Contract into a span."
>
> So strength first made a way;
> Then beauty flow'd, then wisdom, honour,
>   pleasure.
> When almost all was out, God made a stay,
> Perceiving that alone of all his treasure
>   Rest in the bottom lay.
>
> "For if I should" (said he)
> "Bestow this jewel also on my creature,
> He would adore my gifts instead of me,
> And rest in Nature, not the God of Nature;
>   So both should losers be.

"Yet let him keep the rest,
But keep them with repining restlessness;
Let him be rich and weary, that at least,
If goodness lead him not, yet weariness
      May toss him to my breast."

—GEORGE HERBERT

The Lord is my shepherd, I shall not be in want

Come, let us bow down in worship,
    let us kneel before the Lord our Maker;
for he is our God
    and we are the people of his pasture,
    the flock under his care.

—PSALM 95:6–7

The problem with most of us is that we have no clear picture of the God we long to worship. Our image of Him is clouded by the memory of cold cathedrals and bitter religions, by pastors or priests who put the fear of God into us, or by all that we suffered as children from fathers who were absent, emotionally detached, brutal, or weak. All of us have inexact notions of God.

So the question is God Himself: Who is He? This is the question to which all others lead—the question that God Himself put into our hearts (and if He put it into our hearts there must be an answer in His heart waiting to be revealed).

David gives us a comforting and compelling answer: "The LORD is my *shepherd*."

"*Yahweh* is my shepherd" is the word David actually wrote, using the name that God gave Himself. An older generation of scholars referred to the name as the Ineffable Tetragrammaton—the unutterable four-letter word. God's name (written without vowels as YHWH) was rarely pronounced by the Jews for fear of arousing God's wrath. Instead they substituted some lesser word like *Adonai* (my Lord) or *Elohim* (a generic name for God).

The term *Yahweh,* sometimes shortened to *Yah* in the Old Testament, comes from a form of the Hebrew verb *to be* and suggests a self-sufficient God. But that explanation is cold comfort to me. I prefer David's description: Yahweh is my *shepherd.*

Shepherd is a modest metaphor, yet one that is freighted with meaning. Part of the comparison is the portrayal of a shepherd and his sheep; the other is David's experience and ours. David paints a picture and puts us into it. This is the genius of the psalm: It belongs to us; we can use David's words as our own.

David's opening statement, "The LORD is my shepherd," introduces the controlling image that appears throughout the poem. Each line elaborates the symbol, filling out the picture, showing us how our Shepherd-God leads us to that place where we shall no longer want.

The meaning of the metaphor

David himself was a shepherd. He spent much of his youth tending his "few sheep in the desert" (1 Samuel 17:28). The desert is one of the best places in the world to learn. There are few distractions, and there is little that can be used. In such a place we're more inclined to think about the meaning of things rather than about what those things provide.

One day as David was watching his sheep the idea came to him that God is like a shepherd. He thought of the incessant care that sheep require— their helplessness and defenselessness. He recalled their foolish straying from safe paths, their constant need for a guide. He thought of the time and the patience it took for them to trust him before they would follow. He remembered the times when he led them through danger and they huddled close at his heels. He pondered the fact that he must think for his sheep, fight for them, guard them, and find their pasture and quiet pools. He remembered their bruises and scratches that he bound up, and he marveled at how frequently he had to rescue them from harm. Yet not one of his sheep was aware of how well it was watched. Yes, he mused, God is very much like a good shepherd.

Ancient shepherds knew their sheep by name. They were acquainted with all their ways—their peculiarities, their characteristic marks, their tendencies, their idiosyncrasies.

Back then, shepherds didn't drive their sheep, they led them. At the shepherd's morning call—a distinctive guttural sound—each flock would rise and follow its master to the feeding grounds. Even if two shepherds called their flocks at the same time and the sheep were intermingled, they never followed the wrong shepherd. All day long the sheep followed their own shepherd as he searched the wilderness looking for grassy meadows and sheltered pools where his flock could feed and drink in peace.

At certain times of the year it became necessary to move the flocks deeper into the wilderness, a desolate wasteland where predators lurked. But the sheep were always well guarded. Shepherds carried a "rod" (a heavy club) on their belts and a staff in their hands. The shepherd's staff had a crook that was used to remove the sheep from perilous places or to restrain them from wandering away; the club was a weapon to ward off beasts. David said, "When a lion or a bear came and carried off a sheep from the flock, I went after it, . . . and rescued the sheep from its mouth" (1 Samuel 17:34–35).

Throughout the day each shepherd stayed close to his sheep, watching them carefully and protecting them from the slightest harm. When one sheep strayed the shepherd searched for it until it was found. Then he laid it across his shoulders and brought it back home. At the end of the day, each shepherd led his flock to the safety of the fold and slept across the gate to protect them.

A good shepherd *never* left his sheep alone. They would have been lost without him. His presence was their assurance.

It's this good shepherd that David envisioned as he composed each line of his song.

Jacob . . .

The patriarch Jacob was a shepherd and the first person in the Bible to make use of the shepherd metaphor for God. As he lay dying, he looked back over his life and summed it up with these words: "God . . . has been my shepherd all my life" (Genesis 48:15).

Jacob was born with a difficult disposition. Gripping his twin brother's heel at birth, he continued throughout his life to try to trip him up and get ahead of him. In fact, Jacob's whole life was characterized by wheeling, double-dealing, grasping, grabbing, and jerking people around to gain selfish advantage. Yet God was not ashamed to be called "the God of Jacob" and to be his shepherd every day of his life.

Jacob is reminiscent of those who come into life with a pervasive tendency to go wrong: who inhabit inherited hells—saddled from birth with insecurities, insanities, and sinful predilections; who are addicted to food, sex, alcohol, drugs, spending, gambling, or working; who have dis-

turbed and difficult personalities; who have, as
C. S. Lewis said, a "hard machine to drive."

God knows our tiresome stories. He understands the latent forces and all the sources and possibilities of evil in our natures. He sees the hurt and
the heartbreak that others cannot see and which
cannot be explained—even to our closest friends.
He's aware of the reasons for our moodiness, our
temper tantrums, our selfish indulgences. Others
may be put off by our dispositions, but God never
turns away. He sees beyond the prickliness to the
broken heart. His understanding is infinite.

How damaged we are or how far wrong we've
gone are matters of indifference to Him. Our vile-
ness does not alter His character. He is *eternal*
love—the same yesterday, today, forever. We are
not what He wants us to be, but we are not unwant-
ed. If we will have Him, He will be our shepherd.

Frederick Buechner marvels at the folly of God
to welcome "lamebrains and misfits and nit-pickers
and holier than thous and stuffed shirts and odd
ducks and egomaniacs and milquetoasts and closet
sensualists," but that's the way He is. Whatever we
are, wherever we are, His heart is open to us. As
George MacDonald says, "Love surrounds us, seeking
the smallest crack by which it may rush in."

Isn't it odd
That a being like God
Who sees the facade
Still loves the clod
He made out of sod?
Now isn't that odd?

—UNKNOWN

Isaiah . . .

Isaiah envisions a stellar Shepherd who each night calls out His star-flock by name:

Lift your eyes and look to the heavens:
Who created all these?
He who brings out the starry host one by one,
and calls them each by name.
Because of his great power and mighty strength,
not one of them is missing.

—ISAIAH 40:26

It's not by chance that the stars have their assigned orbits and places in the universe. They do not rise at random, nor do they wander haphazardly through space. They rise at God's beck and call: He brings out the starry host one by one and calls

34

them each by name. Not one is forgotten; not one is overlooked; not one is left behind.

It's a terrible thing to be unknown. We live in fear that we will never be known enough—that others will never know who we really are, what our dreams are and where our thoughts are taking us. Yet we have nothing to fear. God knows every one of His sheep by name.

He's aware of each personality and peculiarity: There are the little ones that have to be carried, the cripples that can't keep up, the nursing ewes that won't be hurried, the old sheep that can barely get along. There are the bellwethers that always want to be out front, the bullies that butt and push to get their way, the timid ones (the sheepish) that are afraid to follow, the black sheep that are always the exception. There are those who graze their way into lostness and there are others more deliberately on the lam. The Good Shepherd knows us all.

> The Sovereign LORD comes with power,
> and his arm rules for him. . . .
> He tends his flock like a shepherd:
> He gathers his lambs in his arms
> and carries them close to his heart;
> he gently leads those that have young.
>
> —ISAIAH 40:10–11

God knows our pace. He knows when grief, pain, and loneliness overwhelm us; when the full realization of our limitations comes home to us; when we're shamed and broken and unable to go on. God does not drive His sheep; He gently leads them. He allows for hesitation and trepidation. He gives credit for decisions and resolutions that are strenuously tested; He understands courage that falters in the face of terrible odds; He can accommodate a faith that flames out under stress. He takes into account the hidden reasons for failure; He feels the full weight of our disasters. He knows our pain as no one else knows it. Our bleating reaches His ears; He hears even our inarticulate cries.

When we lag behind He does not scold us. Rather He gathers us up, encircles us with His strong arm, and carries us next to His heart. The essence, the central core of God's character, lies here: He has the heart of a tender shepherd. "Great is the gentleness of our Lord," says German scholar Johann Bengel.

Jeremiah . . .

The prophet Jeremiah saw a flock of ruined sheep.

My people have been lost [ruined] sheep;
    their shepherds have led them astray
    and caused them to roam on the mountains.
They wandered over mountain and hill
    and forgot their own resting place. . . .
But I will bring Israel back to his own pasture.

—JEREMIAH 50:6, 19

We readily forget God, our "resting place," and wander away. Yet He pursues us wherever we go with no complaint of the darkness, the cold wind, the heavy burden, the steep hill, or the thorny path over which He must pass to rescue one lost sheep. His love does not count time, energy, suffering, or even life itself.

"Lord what are those blood drops all the way
That mark out the mountain's track?"
"They were shed for one who had gone astray
Ere the Shepherd could bring him back."
"Lord, why are your hands so rent and torn?"
"They are pierced tonight by many a thorn
They are pierced tonight by many a thorn."

—ELIZABETH CLEPHANE

His pursuit is not a reward for our goodness, but the result of His decision to love. He is driven by love, not by our beauty. He is drawn to us when we have done nothing right and when we have done everything wrong (especially when we have done everything wrong).

"What do you think?" said Jesus, "If a man owns a hundred sheep, and one of them wanders away, will he not leave the ninety-nine on the hills and go to look for the one that wandered off? And if he finds it, I tell you the truth, he is happier about that one sheep than about the ninety-nine that did not wander off. In the same way your Father in heaven is not willing that any of these little ones should be lost" (Matthew 18:12–14).

Lost sheep are not doomed, they're the ones He came to find. "The ambitious, the vain, the highly sexed," said C. H. Sisson, are His "natural prey."

Ezekiel . . .

Ezekiel announced the birth of the Good Shepherd long before He was born. He said that when He came He would tend God's flock with tender, loving care.

> My sheep wandered over all the mountains and on every high hill. They were scattered over the whole earth, and no one searched

or looked for them. . . . For this is what the
Sovereign LORD says: I myself will search
for my sheep and look after them. As a
shepherd looks after his scattered flock
when he is with them, so will I look after
my sheep. I will rescue them from all the
places where they were scattered on a day
of clouds and darkness. . . . I will tend
them in a good pasture. . . . There they will
lie down in good grazing land, and there
they will feed in a rich pasture. . . . I myself
will tend my sheep and have them lie
down, declares the Sovereign LORD. I will
search for the lost and bring back the
strays. I will bind up the injured and
strengthen the weak.

—EZEKIEL 34:6, 11–12, 14–16

It was Ezekiel's task to care for scattered exiles
far from home. He described them as sheep that
were scattered "because there was no shepherd, . . .
and no one searched or looked for them."

Israel's disbanding was their own fault, the
result of years of indifference and resistance to God.
They had looked to their idols, shed blood, defiled
their neighbors' wives, and done other abominable

things (Ezekiel 33:26). That's why they were estranged. Yet, God says, "I will search for the lost and bring back the strays." Good shepherds don't look down on lost sheep; they look *for* them.

Sheep don't have to go looking for their shepherd. It's the other way around: He's out looking for them. Even if the sheep aren't thinking about the shepherd, He pursues them to the ends of the earth:

> He follows them into their own long,
> dark journey; there, where they thought
> finally to escape him, they run straight
> into his arms.
>
> SIMON TUGWELL

There is, in fact, no way to escape Him *except* by running into His arms. Though we are stiff-necked and stubborn, He is equally stiff-necked and stubborn: He will never give up His pursuit. He cannot get us off of His mind.

Furthermore, Ezekiel says, when the Good Shepherd finds His sheep He looks after them: "As a shepherd looks after his scattered sheep when he is with them, so will I look after my sheep."

"Look after" suggests careful examination of each animal. Our Shepherd-God is a good shepherd;

He knows well the condition of His flock; He sees the marks of sorrow on each face. He knows every cut and bruise, every ache and pain. He recognizes the signs of hounding, misuse, and abuse—the wounds that others have given us and the residue of our own resistance.

He promises to do what other shepherds cannot or will not do: "I will bind up the injured and strengthen the weak." He has compassion on the afflicted and the handicapped, on those wounded by their own sin. He understands sorrow, misfortune, broken homes, shattered ambition. He heals the brokenhearted and binds up their wounds (Psalm 147:3). He applies the balm that makes the wounded whole. That's the comfort of God to our beleaguered hearts.

But there is more. Another Good Shepherd was on the way, one who would be one with the Father in pastoral compassion:

> I will place over them one [unique] shepherd, my servant David, and he will tend them; he will tend them and be their shepherd. I the LORD will be their God and my servant David will be a prince among them. I the LORD have spoken.
>
> **EZEKIEL 34:23–24**

Another Good Shepherd: David's long-awaited Son, our Lord Jesus, that Great Shepherd who lays down His life for the sheep (John 10:11).

That Great Shepherd of the sheep

Some six hundred years later Jesus stood near the place where David composed his Shepherd Song and said with quiet assurance,

> I [myself] am the good shepherd. The good shepherd lays down his life for the sheep. The hired hand is not the shepherd who owns the sheep. So when he sees the wolf coming, he abandons the sheep and runs away. Then the wolf attacks the flock and scatters it. The man runs away because he is a hired hand and cares nothing for the sheep.
>
> I am the good shepherd; I know my sheep and my sheep know me—just as the Father knows me and I know the Father—and I lay down my life for the sheep.
>
> —JOHN 10:11–15

This is our Lord Jesus, "that Great Shepherd of the sheep" (Hebrews 13:20).

He was one with the Father. He too saw us as "sheep without a shepherd." He "came to seek and to save what was lost" (Luke 19:10). He's the one who left the "ninety-nine on the hills" and went "to look for the one [sheep] that wandered away," forever establishing the value of one person and the Father's desire that not one of them should be lost (Matthew 18:12–14).

> He has a shepherd's *heart,* beating with pure and generous love that counted not His own life-blood too dear a price to pay down as our ransom. He has a shepherd's *eye,* that takes in the whole flock and misses not even the poor sheep wandering away on the mountains cold. He has a shepherd's *faithfulness,* which will never fail or forsake, leave us comfortless, nor flee when He sees the wolf coming. He has a shepherd's *strength,* so that He is well able to deliver us from the jaw of the lion or the paw of the bear. He has a shepherd's *tenderness*; no lamb so tiny that He will not carry it; no saint so weak that He will not gently lead; no soul so faint that He will not give it rest. . . . His gentleness makes great.
>
> —F. B. MEYER

But there's more: The Good Shepherd laid down His life for the sheep. The Father issued the decree: "Awake, O sword, against my shepherd, against the man who is close to me! . . . Strike the shepherd" (Zechariah 13:7). And the Shepherd was slain.

Since the beginning of time religions have decreed that a lamb should give up its life for the shepherd. The shepherd would bring his lamb to the sanctuary, lean with all his weight on the lamb's head, and confess his sin. The lamb would be slain and its blood would flow out—a life for a life.

What irony: Now the Shepherd gives up His life for His lamb. "He was pierced for *our* transgressions, he was crushed for *our* iniquities; the punishment that brought us peace was upon him, and by his wounds we are healed. We all, like sheep, have gone astray, each of us has turned to his own way; and the LORD has laid on him the iniquity of us all" (Isaiah 53:5–6).

We may not know; we cannot tell
What pains he had to bear,
But we believe it was for us
He hung and suffered there.

—CECIL F. ALEXANDER

The story is about the death of God. "He himself bore our sins in his body on the tree, so that we might die to sins and live for righteousness; by his wounds you have been healed" (1 Peter 2:24). He died for *all* sin—the obvious sins of murder, adultery, and theft, as well as for the secret sins of selfishness and pride. He *Himself* bore our sins in His body on the cross. This was sin's final cure.

The normal way of looking at the Cross is to say that man was so bad and God was so mad that someone had to pay. But it was not anger that led Christ to be crucified; it was love. The Crucifixion is the point of the story: God loves us so much that He *Himself* took on our guilt. He internalized *all* our sin and healed it. When it was over He said, "It is finished!" There is nothing left for us to do but to enter into forgiving acceptance—and for those of us who have already entered it, to enter into more of it.

The Shepherd calls to us and listens for the slightest sounds of life. He hears the faintest cry. If He hears nothing at all, He will not give up or go away. He lets us wander away, hoping that weariness and despair will turn us around.

For all
who knew the shelter of The Fold,
its warmth and safety
and The Shepherd's care,
and bolted;
choosing instead to fare
out in the cold,
the night;
revolted
by guardianship,
by Light;
lured
by the unknown;
eager to be out
and on their own;
freed
to water where they may,
feed where they can,
live as they will:
till
they are cured,
let them be cold,
ill;
let them know terror;
feed
them with thistle,
weed,
and thorn;
who chose

the company of wolves,
let them taste
the companionship wolves give
to helpless strays;
but, oh! let them live—
wiser though torn!
And wherever
however far away
they roam,
follow
and
watch
and
keep
Your stupid, wayward, stubborn sheep,
and someday
bring them Home!

—RUTH BELL GRAHAM

Our discomfort is God's doing: He hounds us; He hems us in; He thwarts our dreams; He foils our best-laid plans; He frustrates our hopes; He waits until we know that nothing will ease our pain, nothing will make life worth living except His presence. And when we turn to Him, He is there to greet us. He has been there all along. "The LORD is near to all who call on him" (Psalm 145:18).

But you say, Why would He want me? He knows my sin, my wandering, my long habits of yielding. I'm not good enough. I'm not sorry enough for my sin. I'm unable not to sin.

Our waywardness doesn't have to be explained to God. He's never surprised by anything we do. He sees everything at a single glance—what is, what could have been, what would have been apart from our sinful choices. He sees into the dark corners and crannies of our hearts and knows everything about us there is to know. But what He sees only draws out His love. There is no deeper motivation in God than love. It is His nature to love; He can do no other. "God is love" (1 John 4:8).

Do you have some nameless grief? Some vague, sad pain? Some inexplicable ache in your heart? Come to Him who made your heart. Jesus said, "Come to me, all you who are weary and burdened, and I will give you rest. Take my yoke upon you and learn from me, for I am gentle and humble in heart, and you will find rest for your souls. For my yoke is easy and my burden is light" (Matthew 11:28–30).

To know that God is like this, and to know this God, is rest. There is no more profound lesson than this: He is the one thing that we need.

The King of Love my Shepherd is,
  Whose goodness faileth never;
I nothing lack if I am His,
  And He is mine forever.

—HENRY W. BAKER

The LORD is my shepherd . . .

Shepherd—the word carries with it thoughts of tenderness, security, and provision, yet it means nothing as long as I cannot say, "The Lord is *my* shepherd."

What a difference that monosyllable makes—all the difference in the world. It means that I can have all of God's attention, all of the time, just as though I'm the only one. I may be part of a flock, but I'm one of a kind.

It's one thing to say, "The Lord is a shepherd"; it's another to say, "The Lord is *my* shepherd." Martin Luther observed that faith is a matter of personal pronouns: *My* Lord and *my* God. This is the faith that saves.

Every morning the Shepherd "calls his own sheep by name and leads them out. When he has brought out all his own, he goes on ahead of them, and his sheep follow him because they know his voice" (John 10:3–4).

This morning as you awakened, His eyes swept over you, He called you by name and said, "Come, follow Me." It's a once-for-all thing; it's an everyday thing.

Let not conscience make you linger,
Nor of fitness fondly dream,
All the fitness he requireth,
Is to feel your need of him.

—JOSEPH HART

HE MAKES ME LIE DOWN IN GREEN PASTURES, HE LEADS ME BESIDE QUIET WATERS

O happy field wherein
This fodder grew
Whose taste doth us
from beasts to
men renew.

—ROBERT SOUTHWELL

LEFT TO OURSELVES WE WOULD HAVE NOTHING MORE than restlessness, driven by the realization that there is something more to know and love. But God will not leave us to ourselves. He *makes* us lie down in green pastures. He *leads* us by quiet waters.

The verbs suggest gentle persuasion—a shepherd patiently, persistently encouraging his sheep to the place where their hungers and thirsts will be assuaged.

In David's day "green pastures" were oases, verdant places in the desert toward which shepherds led their thirsty flocks. Left to themselves sheep would wander off into the wilderness and die. Experienced shepherds knew the terrain and urged their flocks toward familiar grasslands and streams where they could forage and feed, lie down and rest.

The picture here is not of sheep grazing and drinking, but of sheep at rest, lying down—literally, "stretched out." The verb *leads* suggests a slow and leisurely pace. The scene is one of tranquility, satisfaction, and rest.

The common practice of shepherds was to graze their flocks in rough pasture early in the morning, leading them to better grasses as the morning progressed, and then coming to a cool and shaded oasis for noontime rest.

The image of placid waters emphasizes the concept of rest—the condition of having all our passions satisfied. Augustine cried out, "What will *make* me take my rest in you . . . so I can forget my restlessness and take hold of you, the one good thing in my life?"

The compulsion begins with God. "*He* makes me [*causes* me to] lie down in green pastures, *He* leads me beside still waters." "He calls his own sheep by name and leads them out. When he has brought out all his own, he goes on ahead of them, and the sheep follow him because they know his voice" (John 10:3–4).

God makes the first move; He takes the initiative—calling us, leading us to a place of rest.

It's not that we're seeking God; He is seeking us. "There is a property in God of thirst and longing . . ." says Dame Julian of Norwich, "he hath longing to have us."

God's cry to wayward Adam and Eve, "Where are you?" (Genesis 3:9) suggests the loneliness He feels when separated from those He loves. G. K. Chesterton suggests that the whole Bible is about the "loneliness of God." I like the thought that in some inexplicable way God misses me, that He can't bear to be separated from me, that I'm always on His mind, that He patiently, insistently calls me, seeks me, not for my own sake alone, but for His. He cries, "Where are you?"

Deep within us is a place for God. We were made for God and without His love we ache in loneliness and emptiness. He calls from deep space to our depths: "Deep calls to deep" (Psalm 42:7).

David put it this way, "My heart says of you, 'Seek his face!' Your face, LORD, I will seek" (Psalm 27:8). God spoke to the depths of David's heart, uttering His heart's desire: "Seek my face." And David responded with alacrity, "I will seek your face, Lord."

And so it is: God calls us—seeking us to seek Him—and our hearts resonate with longing for Him.

That understanding has radically changed the way I look at my relationship to God. It is now neither duty nor discipline—a regimen I impose on myself like a hundred sit-ups and fifty push-ups each day—but a response, an answer, to one who has been calling me all my life.

> *I sought the Lord, and afterward I knew*
> *He moved my soul to seek Him, seeking me;*
> *It was not I that found, O Savior true,*
> *No, I was found of Thee.*
>
> —GEORGE MACDONALD

Taking God in

But what are those green pastures and quiet waters to which He leads us? And where are they? What is the reality behind these metaphors?

The real thing is God Himself. *He is* our true pasture (Jeremiah 50:7) and our pool of quiet water. He is our true nourishment, our living water. If we do not take Him in we will starve.

There is a hunger in the human heart that nothing but God can satisfy. There is a thirst that no one but He can quench. "Fiercely we dig the fountain, to know the water true," but there's no satisfaction until we come to Him. "Do not work for food that spoils," Jesus said, "but for food that endures to eternal life, which the Son of Man will give you. . . . I am the bread of life. He who comes to me will *never* go hungry, and he who believes in me will *never* be thirsty" (John 6:27, 35).

Malcolm Muggeridge's confession is a striking expression of this thought:

> I may, I suppose, regard myself as being a relatively successful man. People occasionally look at me on the street. That's fame. I can fairly easily earn enough to qualify for the highest slopes of inland revenue. That's success. Furnished with money and a little fame, even the elderly, if they care to, can partake of trendy diversions. That's pleasure. It might happen once in a while that

something I said or wrote was sufficiently heeded to persuade myself that it represented a serious impact on our time. That's fulfillment. Yet I say to you, and I beg of you to believe me, multiply these tiny triumphs by a million, add them all together, and they are nothing, less than nothing, a positive impediment, measured against one draught of that living water that is offered to the spiritually hungry.

Grazing on God; drinking Him in . . .

But how do we graze on God? How do we drink Him in? Once more we're confronted with symbolism. What do the metaphors mean?

The process begins, as all relationships do, with a meeting. As David said:

As the deer pants for streams of water,
    so my soul pants for you, O God.
My soul thirsts . . . for the living God.
    When can I go and meet with God?

—PSALM 42:1–2

God is a real person. He is not a human invention, a concept, a theory, or a projection of ourselves. He is overwhelmingly alive—real beyond our wildest dreams. He can be "met," to translate David's commonplace word.

A. W. Tozer wrote,

> God is a Person and as such can be culti-
> vated as any person can. God is a Person
> and in the depths of his mighty nature he
> thinks, wills, enjoys, feels, loves, desires
> and suffers as any other person may. God is
> a Person and can be known in increasing
> degrees of intimacy as we prepare our
> hearts for the wonder of it.

There's the reality, but there's also the rub: Are we willing to prepare ourselves to meet Him? He responds to the slightest approach, but we're only as close as we want to be. "If . . . you seek the LORD your God, you will find him," Moses promised, then added this proviso: "if you look for him with all your heart and with all your soul" (Deuteronomy 4:29).

We don't have to look very hard or very long for God. He's only as far away as our hearts (Romans 10:8–9), but He will not intrude. He calls us but then waits for our answer. Our progress toward Him is determined by our desire to engage Him in a personal way—to *know* Him.

We say, "Something's wrong with me; I'm not happy; there must be something more," but we do nothing about our discontent. It's this mood of resignation that keeps us from joy. Our first task is to get honest with ourselves. Do we want God or not? If we do, we must be willing to make the effort to respond to Him. "Come near to God," says James "and he will come near to you" (James 4:8). It's a matter of desire. "O God, you are my God, *earnestly* I seek you," the psalmist says (Psalm 63:1).

Solitude

"Begin small and start promptly," is an old Quaker saying. The idea is to keep things simple and to begin now. Simplicity begins with solitude—not mere time alone, but time alone with God.

> Solitude begins with a time and place for God, and him alone. If we really believe not only that God exists, but that he is actively present in our lives—healing, teaching, and guiding—we need to set aside a time and space to give him our undivided attention.
>
> —HENRI NOUWEN

But where can we find that solitude? Where can we find a quiet place in the midst of the din and demands of this world? "In a crowd it's difficult to see God," Augustine said, "This vision craves secret retirement." "Go into your room," Jesus said, "close your door and pray to your Father, who is unseen" (Matthew 6:6).

There is a meeting place—a time and place where we can meet with God and hear His thoughts and He can hear ours, a time for the two of us where He can have our full attention and we can have His.

Solitude is where we are least alone and where our deepest loneliness can be relieved. It's a healing place where God can repair the damage done by the noise and pressure of the world. "The more you visit it," Thomas á Kempis said, "the more you will want to return."

> *You have to get up arly,*
> *Ef you want to take in God . . .*
>
> —JAMES RUSSELL LOWELL

"I will awaken the dawn," says David (Psalm 57:8). There's something to be said for meeting God before our busy days begin and our schedules begin to tyrannize us, though we must not understand this in some legalistic way to mean we have to get up before the sun to merit a meeting with God. For many, morning is the most opportune time; for others, it's more of an opportunity for the devil. There are times when it not only *seems* easier to meet with God, it *is* easier. It's something you have to work out with your body. The main thing is eagerness to meet Him. The advantage of doing so early is that we hear His thoughts before other thoughts invade our minds.

The first step is to find a Bible, a quiet place, and an uninterrupted period of time. Sit quietly and remind yourself that you're in the presence of God. He is there with you, eager to meet with you. "Stay in that secret place," A. W. Tozer said, "till the surrounding noises begin to fade out of your heart, till a sense of God's presence has enveloped you. Listen for His inward voice till you learn to recognize it."

Until we take time to be quiet we'll not hear God. God cannot be heard in noise and restlessness, only in silence. He will speak to us if we will give Him a chance, if we will listen, if we will be quiet. "Be still," the psalmist sings, "and know that I am God" (Psalm 46:10).

"*Listen, listen* to me," God pleads, "and eat what is good, and your soul will delight in the richest of fare. Give ear and come to me; hear me, that your soul may live" (Isaiah 55:2–3).

Listen to Him. There's no other way to take Him in. "When your words came, I ate them" said Jeremiah (Jeremiah 15:16). Sit at His feet and let Him feed you. That's the place to be (Luke 10:38–42).

> *Better than thrill a listening crowd*
> *Sit at a wise man's feet.*
>
> —GEORGE MACDONALD

The problem with many of us is that, though we read God's Word, we're not feeding on God. We're more intent on mastering the text—finding out its precise meaning, gathering theories and theologies—so we can talk more intelligently about God. The main purpose of reading the Bible, however, is not to accumulate data about Him, but to come to Him, to encounter Him as our living God.

> *You are not here to verify,*
> *instruct yourself, or inform curiosity,*
> *Or carry report. You are here to kneel.*
>
> —T. S. ELIOT

Jesus said to the best-read Bible students of His day, "You diligently study the Scriptures because you think that by them you possess eternal life. These are the Scriptures that testify about me" (John 5:39).

The scholars read the Bible, but they didn't listen to God; they never heard His voice. We should do more than read words; we should seek "the Word exposed in the words," as Karl Barth said. We want to move beyond information to seeing God and being informed and shaped by His truth. There's a passing exhilaration—the joy of discovery—in acquiring knowledge about the Bible, but there's no life in it. The Bible is not an end in itself, but a stimulus to our interaction with God.

Start with a conscious desire to engage Him in a personal way. Select a portion of Scripture—a verse, a paragraph, a chapter—and read it over and over. Think of Him as present and speaking to you, disclosing His mind and emotions and will. God is articulate. He speaks to us through His Word. Meditate on His words until His thoughts begin to take shape in your mind.

Thoughts is exactly the right word because that's precisely what the Bible is—the *mind* of the Lord" (see 1 Corinthians 2:6–16). When we read His Word we are reading His mind—what He knows, what He feels, what He wants, what He enjoys, what He desires, what He loves, what He hates.

Take time to reflect on what He is saying. Think about each word. Give yourself time for prayerful contemplation until God's heart is revealed and your heart is exposed.

> Read quietly, slowly, word for word to enter into the subject more with the heart than with the mind. From time to time make short pauses to allow these truths time to flow through all the recesses of the soul.
>
> —JEAN-PIERRE DE CAUSSADE

Listen carefully to the words that touch your emotions, and meditate on His goodness. Feed on His faithfulness (Psalm 37:3). Think about His kindness and those glimpses of His unfailing love that motivate you to love Him more (Psalm 48:9). Savor His words. "*Taste* and see that the LORD is good" (Psalm 34:8).

> Spend one hour a day in adoration of the Lord and you'll be all right.
>
> —MOTHER TERESA

Mother Teresa might say something different to you and me. So much depends on our temperament, our family and job demands, the state of our health, our age and level of maturity. At first ten or fifteen minutes may be all we can manage. Then perhaps we will be ready for an hour every day. It's not important how much time we spend at first. The important thing is to make a beginning. God's Spirit will let us know where to go from there.

Our reading should be toward relishing God, delighting in Him, gazing at His beauty, as David said (Psalm 27:4). When we approach God in that way it inclines us to want more of Him. "I have tasted Thee," Augustine said, "and now I hunger for Thee."

There's no need to worry about texts that we don't understand. Some meanings will escape us. Everything difficult indicates something more than our hearts can yet embrace. As Jesus said to His disciples, "I have much more to say to you, more than you can now bear" (John 16:12). There's much that we will never know, but some of the hard questions will be answered when we're ready for them.

God can never be understood through the intellect. Insight arises from purity of heart—from love, humility, and a desire to obey. It's the pure in heart who see God, Jesus said (Matthew 5:8). The more of God's truth we know and want to obey the more we know.

> The words of the Lord are seeds sown in
> our hearts by the sower. They have to fall
> into our hearts to grow. Meditation and
> prayer must water them and obedience
> keep them in the light. Thus they will bear
> fruit for the Lord's gathering.
>
> —GEORGE MACDONALD

Nor should we worry about our doubts. How could God possibly reveal Himself in a way that would leave no room for doubt?

Madeleine L'Engle said, "Those who believe they believe in God . . . without anguish of mind, without uncertainty, without doubt, and even at times without despair, believe only in the idea of God, and not in God himself."

Uncertainty is the name of the game. The best thing is to take our questionings and doubts directly to God, as David often did. His psalms are filled with discomfort and disagreement with God's ways. He fills page after page with confusion and disbelief. It's good to do so. God can handle our hesitancy.

Sometimes we're mentally dull or emotionally flat, weary, and tired. On such occasions it's worthless to try to make ourselves think more deeply or respond more intensely. If the value of our times alone with God depend on our emotional state, we will always be troubled. We should never worry about how we feel. Even when our minds are confused or our hearts are cold we can learn from our solitude. Don't try to make your heart love God. Just give it to Him.

If we're having a hard time with God, if we don't yet trust His heart, we should read the Gospels—Matthew, Mark, Luke, and John. There we hear what Jesus said and did and what was said about Him. There we see Him making visible the invisible God. When Philip, Jesus' disciple, asked to see God, Jesus replied, "Don't you know me, Philip, even after I have been among you such a long time? Anyone who has seen me has seen the Father. How can you say, 'Show us the Father'?" (John 14:9). Philip's request

is the profound expression of deep hunger behind the whole religious quest, speaking for saints and mystics, thinkers, moralists and men of faith of every age. "He that hath seen me hath seen the Father,' is Christ's staggering response. That is what the doctrine of Christ's divine Sonship really means, and why it matters. In His words we hear God speaking; in His deeds we see God at work; in His reproach we glimpse God's judgment; in His love we feel God's heart beating. If this be not true, we know nothing of God at all. If it be true—and we know it is—then . . . Jesus is God manifest in the flesh, the unique, incomparable, only begotten Son of the Living God.

—UNKNOWN

The main use of the Gospels is to help us see the character of God made real, personal, and understandable in Jesus. What we see Jesus doing—caring, suffering, weeping, calling, seeking—is what God is doing and has been doing all along. If you can't love God try to see Him in Jesus. There, He's revealed as one who has no limits to His love; one to whom we can come with all our doubts, disappointments, and misjudgments; one "whom we can approach without fear and to whom we can submit ourselves without despair" (Blaise Pascal). In the Gospels we see that God is the only God worth having.

And then to pray . . .

As we listen to God we should answer. This is prayer—our response to the revelation and unfolding of God's heart. "My God, Thy creature answers Thee," said the French poet Mussett. Prayer, understood in that way, is an extension of our visits with God rather than something tacked on.

Our meetings with God are like a polite conversation with a friend. They're not monologues in which one person does all the talking and the other does all the listening, but dialogues in which we listen thoughtfully to one another's self-disclosure and then respond.

One of my colleagues describes the process this way: If we're reading a note from a loved one in which we're praised, loved, appreciated, counseled, corrected, and helped in various ways and that individual is present in the room while we read, it's only right that we should express thanks, reciprocate love, ask questions, and in other ways react to the message. It would be rude to do otherwise. This is prayer.

Around 1370 a book was published with the title *The Cloud of Unknowing*. It's thought that the author was a spiritual director in a monastery, but we don't know his name. Much of what he wrote is hard to understand, but when it comes to prayer he was profoundly simple.

God, he said, can be known, even through "the cloud of unknowing" by responding to Him with "just a little word . . . the shorter it is the better." His book is a textbook of succinct and simple prayer:

> It is good to think of your kindness, O God
>   and to love you and praise you for that.
> Yet it is far better to think
>   upon your simple being,
> and to love you and praise you
>   for yourself.
> Lord, I covet you and seek you
>   and nothing but you.
>
> My God,
>   you are all I need, and more;
> whoever has you needs nothing else
>   in this life.

If you don't know where to start, pray David's psalms. David's life was characterized by prayer—"I am a man of prayer," he said (Psalm 109:4). The translators supply *a man of*, but the text reads simply,

"I am prayer." Prayer was the essence of David's life and his genius, as it is ours. We have this access to God, this intimacy with Him, this opportunity to receive all that the heart of God has stored up for us. It is the means by which we receive God's gifts, the means by which everything is done. David teaches us to pray.

Prayer is worship. Our praying should be full of adoration, affection, and fondness for God—that He is who He is; that He created us in order to have someone on whom He could shower His love; that He stretched out His arms on the cross; that He intends, in the fullest sense, to make whole men and women out of us. In worship, as the old word *worth-ship* implies, we declare what we value the most. It is one of the best ways in the world to love God.

Prayer is the highest expression of our dependence on God. It is asking for what we want. We can ask for anything—even the most difficult things. "Do not be anxious about anything, but in everything, by prayer and petition, with thanksgiving, present your requests to God" (Philippians 4:6). Anything large enough to occupy our minds is large enough to hang a prayer on.

Prayer, however, by its nature is *requesting*. It is not insisting or clamoring. We can make no demands

70

of God and no deals with Him. Furthermore, we're coming to a friend. Friends don't make demands. They ask and then wait. We wait with patience and submission until God gives us what we request—or something more.

David wrote, "I have stilled and quieted my soul; like a weaned child with its mother, like a weaned child is my soul within me" (Psalm 131:2). David was in exile, waiting for God, learning not to worry himself with God's delays and other mysterious ways. No longer restless and craving, he waited for God to answer in His own time and in His own way. He is *able* to do far more than anything we can ask or imagine, but He must do it in His time and in His way. We ask in our time and in our way; God answers in His.

Prayer is asking for understanding. It is the means by which we comprehend what God is saying to us in His Word. The process by which we gain awareness of His mind is not natural, but supernatural; spiritual things are discerned spiritually (1 Corinthians 2:6–16). There is truth that can never be grasped by the human intellect. It cannot be discovered; it must be disclosed. Certainly we can understand the facts in the Bible apart from God's help, but we can never plumb its depths, never fully appreciate "what God has prepared for those who love him" (1 Corinthians 2:9). We must pray and wait for truth to come honestly into our minds.

Prayer moves what we know from our heads to our hearts; it's our hedge against hypocrisy, the way by which we begin to ring true. Our perception of truth is always ahead of our condition. Prayer brings us more into conformity; it bridges the gap between what we know and what we are.

Prayer focuses and unites our fragmented hearts. We have a thousand necessities. It's impossible for us to purify them and simplify them and integrate them into one. David prayed: "Give me an undivided heart" (Psalm 86:11). He wanted to love God with his whole soul, but he couldn't sustain the effort. Other interests and affections pulled him and divided him, so he asked God to guard his heart and unite its affections into one.

Satisfied in the morning . . .

> He wakens me morning by morning,
>   wakens my ear to listen like one being
>   taught.

The Sovereign LORD has opened my ears,
    and I have not been rebellious;
    I have not drawn back.
                                    —ISAIAH 50:4

Centering on God has to be done each morning as though it had never been done before. In that quiet place He comforts us, He instructs us, He listens to us, He prepares our hearts and strengthens us for the day. There we learn to love Him and worship Him again; we esteem His words and defer to Him once more; we get His fresh perspective on the problems and possibilities of our day.

Satisfy us in the morning with your unfailing love,
    that we may sing for joy and be glad all our days.
                                    —PSALM 90:14

Then we should take His presence with us all through the day—journeying, pausing, waiting, listening, recalling what He said to us in the morning. He is our teacher, our philosopher, our friend; our gentlest, kindest, most interesting companion.

He is with us wherever we go; He is in the commonplace, whether we know it or not. "Surely the LORD is in this place," Jacob said of a most unlikely location, "and I was not aware of it" (Genesis 28:16). We may not realize that He is close by. We may feel lonely and sad and desolate. Our day may seem bleak and dreary without a visible ray of hope, yet He is present. God has said,

> Never will I leave you
>> never will I forsake you.
>
> —HEBREWS 13:5

So we can say with confidence . . .

> The Lord is my helper;
>> I will not be afraid.
>
> —HEBREWS 13:6

The clamor of this visible and audible world is so persistent and God's quiet voice sometimes is so faint that we forget that He is near. But do not worry: He cannot forget us.

> *How oft I wake and find I*
>> *have been forgetting Thee.*
> *I am never far from Thy mind;*
> *Thou it is that wakest me.*
>
> —GEORGE MACDONALD

In God's presence there is satisfaction: His lush meadows are boundless; His still water runs deep. "There," I say to myself, "[I] will lie down in good grazing land, and there [I] will feed in a rich pasture" (Ezekiel 34:14).

HE RESTORES MY SOUL. HE GUIDES ME IN PATHS OF RIGHTEOUSNESS FOR HIS NAME'S SAKE

Virtuous and vicious every man must be,
Few in the extreme, but all in the degree.

—ALEXANDER POPE

GOD KNOWS WE NEED RESTORATION. In the face of common temptation we fall—voluntarily and repeatedly. The same old flaws and failures pursue us all through life. New vices awaken and dominate us. We stumble again and again into bad judgment.

Now and then we set out to restore ourselves. Perhaps, we say, this is the day I will deal
with my jealousy, hate, and lust; I'll find a way
around my self-pity, self-defensiveness, self-
indulgence, and all the other permutations and
hyphenations of self-love that separate us from
God and from one another.

Perhaps, perhaps, but probably not. Despite
these periodic fits of morality, nothing enduring
gets done. Sin remains our sullen master—
untamed and intractable.

We blame bad genes, dysfunctional families,
or demented ancestors, but no one ever has to
push us into wrongdoing; we go all by ourselves.

> *[God] calls thee to cope with enemies; and first*
> *Points out a conflict with thyself—the worst.*
>
> —WILLIAM COWPER

Theologians write about *original sin,* which
might suggest that we sin in novel, creative ways.
But there are no innovative ways to sin. It's all been
done before. No, *original sin* simply means that
we're sinful in our *origins*—"sinful from birth, sinful
from the time my mother conceived me" (Psalm
51:5). We are thrown into this world like a baseball

78

with a spin on it; in time we break and the curve is always down and away.

Total depravity is the other term theologians use to describe our state. It means that sin affects the totality of our beings. If sin were blue, we'd be some shade of blue all over. In one way or another, small or great, hidden or revealed, we're tinted and tainted by sin. Sin is biologic—inborn and immutable—a painful reality manifested in the things we do. We're sinful in the core of our beings—not misguided or mistreated. There is something in our makeup that is dreadfully wrong; it makes us desire wrong, causes us to do wrong, and when we try not to do it, it makes it impossible for us to not think about doing wrong.

But then, we don't have to be told that we're defective. Who of us can say, "I have been blameless . . . and have kept myself from sin" (Psalm 18:23)? No, we need only to be reminded, not told. We know what we're like, though we dislike exposing what we're like to others. As Shakespeare put it, our best conscience is not so much to leave sin undone as it is to keep it unknown.

God, however, won't let us keep it unknown. He permits us to do the most embarrassing things at the most inopportune times—crass, unprincipled acts that shame us to tears. "God does not leave us until he has broken our hearts and our bones" (the Shepherd of Hermes).

> *But to remind us of our, and Adam's curse*
> *And that to be restored, our sickness must get*
> *worse.*
>
> —T. S. ELIOT

We must get worse, it seems, before we can get better. We must experience the depths of our depravity and see the miserable stuff of which we're made.

"No man is really any good," says G. K. Chesterton's detective, Father Brown, "until he knows how bad he is; till he's realized exactly how much right he has to all this snobbery, and sneering, and talking about 'criminals' as if they were apes in a forest ten thousand miles away; till he's got rid of all the dirty self-deception of talking about low types and deficient skulls; till he's squeezed out of his soul the last drop of the oil of the Pharisees; till his only hope is somehow or other to have captured one criminal, and kept him safe and sane under his own hat."

Sin is an atrocity. We have to realize how monstrous and scandalous it is and how desperately we need God's forgiveness. We cannot appreciate the magnitude of His acceptance until we comprehend the measure of our sins. We understand and hunger for His grace only at the point of deep and depressing failure.

David knew God's ways. Never has anyone been so ruthlessly revealed. You know the story about how he fell for Uriah's pretty, young wife, Bathsheba. One brief spell of passionate indulgence and David was plunged into ruin. Judah's illustrious ruler, the sweet singer of Israel, became David, the seducer, the adulterer—then a monstrous liar, a murderer, and then a mass murderer, utterly pitiless and unmoved by his horrifying evil. There's no end to sin once we begin.

Moral collapse is seldom a blowout. It's more like a slow leak, the result of a thousand small indulgences, the consequences of which are not immediately apparent. We are seduced by sin's attraction and led on by subtle degrees. We transition into failure:

> *Vice is a monster of so frightful mien*
> *As, to be hated, needs but to be seen;*
> *Yet seen too oft, familiar with her face,*
> *We first endure, then pity, then embrace.*

—ALEXANDER POPE

The attraction becomes fantasy. (Fictional sin seems exciting while fictional good seems dull. That's the fundamental deception of our fantasies.) Fantasy softens us, and our convictions erode. We're then in a frame of mind to listen to our passions and having listened we have no will to resist.

Then comes the yielding and with the yielding the rationalizations. We have to justify our behavior to ourselves and to others. Everything but our own wrongdoing becomes our reason. All our actions must be explained and made to look good.

But our hearts know. There are moments when our wills soften and we long to set things right. If we do not then listen to our hearts there is a metallic hardening and then corruption. Our wrongdoing mutates, altering its form and quality, evolving into dark narcissism and horrifying cruelty: We don't care who gets hurt as long as we get what we want.

And ultimately there is disclosure. Sooner or later we face the horrible experience of being found out. At first we vehemently deny any wrongdoing. Then we dissemble. (People in trouble always lie.) But inevitably our dishonor is shouted from the housetops. There's no place to hide from the shame. We experience the force of inexorable law: Sin, no matter what we do, will not prosper.

Eventually the consequences catch up to us and we have to face the facts, or, like David, we have to face someone who digs up the facts. Nathan, an old and trusted friend, trapped the shepherd-king with a story about a rich man who seized another man's pet lamb to serve to a "traveling stranger," Nathan's metaphor for David's transient passion (2 Samuel 12:1–4).

David, weary of warding off his conscience, flamed out his verdict on the man and his terrible deed: "As surely as the LORD lives, the man who did this deserves to die! He must pay for that lamb four times over, because he did such a thing and had no pity" (12:5). Sheep-stealing was not a capital offense in Israel. According to Israelite law a thief was only required to make fourfold restitution to the victim (Exodus 22:1). David was overreacting, expending on another the stern judgment he should have applied to himself.

"You are the man!" Nathan said, pointing his finger at David. "This is what the LORD, the God of Israel, says: 'I anointed you king over Israel, and I delivered you from the hand of Saul. I gave your master's house to you, and your master's wives into your arms. I gave you the house of Israel and Judah. And if all this had been too little I would have given you more. Why did you despise the word of the LORD by doing what is evil in his eyes?" (2 Samuel 12:7–9).

Brought face-to-face with his corruption, David buried his face in his hands. "I have sinned against the Lord," was his only reply. No excuses, no justification, no extenuating circumstances, no special pleading. And Nathan said, "The LORD has taken away your sin. You are not going to die" (12:13).

God lets us fall not to shame us, but to assure us that though we are guilty, vile, and helpless we are deeply loved by God. God's love in the face of our wickedness is what awakens us to humility and contrition.

Humility and contrition are the keys to the heart of God. Those who cry out, "God, have mercy on me, a sinner," go home justified (Luke 18:13–14). God has never yet despised a broken and contrite heart (Psalm 51:17).

At the moment of exposure and brokenness, our shame can be driven underground, or we can be touched at the heart level by God's amazing grace and know that though we are miserable sinners we are fully accepted. God loves us though we are lost in sin and confusion. God isn't looking for a few good people: "He instructs *sinners* in his ways" (Psalm 25:8).

David uttered his confession and was interrupted with an outpouring of his Father's forgiveness and love. There was not a moment's interval between his acknowledgment of sin and Nathan's assurance that all was well. Though David bore the consequences of his sin, God canceled the guilt that was against him. He could lift up his head. He could forgive himself and forget himself because of the healing experience of God's love.

When Nathan had gone, David poured out his heart to God,

> Blessed is the man
> > whose transgressions are forgiven,
> > whose sins are covered.
> Blessed is the man
> > whose sin the LORD does not count against
> > > him
> > and in whose spirit is no deceit. . . .
> I acknowledged my sin to you,
> > and did not cover up my iniquity
> I said, "I will confess my transgression to the
> > LORD"—
> > and you forgave the guilt of my sin.

—PSALM 32:1–2, 5

It was the story of the lamb—a little, innocent lamb—that broke David's heart, showed him how great a sinner he was, and brought him to repentance (2 Samuel 12:1–13). And "it is nothing more, and nothing less, than the story of the death of a Lamb, God's lamb, the Lamb of God, slain from the foundation of the world, that brings us to repentance, shows us how great our sin is and how much greater is God's forgiveness" (Clarence E. Macartney).

God stays with us despite our ruin; He discerns the possibilities even in our defilement. He uses our sin to awaken our need for His grace. Sin softens us and makes us more susceptible to His shaping. When we fall, we have fallen into His hands.

"Sin is dark, dangerous, damnable," F. B. Meyer wrote, "but it cannot staunch the love of God; it cannot change the fact of a love that is not of yesterday, but dates from eternity itself."

Rather than mourn our humiliation, we must accept God's grace and His offer of forgiveness and then move on. "By sorrow of heart the spirit is broken," says an old proverb (Proverbs 15:13, KJV).

We must not let sorrow and self-pity set us up! It will break us in the end. We must forget "our own paltry self with its well-earned disgrace, and lift up our eyes to the glory which alone will quicken us" (George MacDonald).

Sin may have consequences with which we must live, but sin acknowledged and confessed can only work for good. It is, in fact, one means by which God shapes us into His image.

> *I asked the Lord that I may grow*
> *in faith and love and every grace,*
> *Might more of his salvation know,*
> *and seek more earnestly his face.*
>
> *'Twas He who taught me thus to pray,*
> *and He I trust has answered prayer,*
> *But it has been in such a way*
> *as almost drove me to despair.*
>
> *I thought that in some favored hour,*
> *at once He'd answer my request,*
> *And by His love's transforming power,*
> *Subdue my sins and give me rest.*
>
> *Instead of that He made me feel*
> *the hidden evils of my heart,*
> *And bade the angry powers of hell*
> *assault my soul in every part.*

Nay, more, with His hand He seemed
    intent to aggravate my woe,
Crossed all the fair designs I schemed,
    blasted my gourds, and laid me low.

"Lord, why this?" I trembling cried.
    "Wilt Thou pursue this worm to death?"
"This is the way," the Lord replied,
    "I answer prayer for grace and faith."

"These inward trials I employ
    from sin and self to set thee free,
And cross thy schemes of earthly joy
    that thou might find thy all in Me."

—JOHN NEWTON

God's love at work . . .

"Even from my sin," said Augustine, "God draws good."

God's love in the face of our sin is what causes us to long for His righteousness. His love softens our hearts, draws us to repentance, and makes us hungry for righteousness. It is the love of God and His goodness to us that draws us to repentance.

Brennan Manning said it well:

When I am in conscious communion with the reality of the wild, passionate, relentless, stubborn, pursuing, tender love of God for me, then it's not that I have to or I got to or I must or I should or I ought; suddenly, I want to change because I know how deeply I'm loved. One of the wonderful results of my consciousness of God's staggering love for me as I am is a freedom not to be who I should be or who others want me to be. I can be who I really am. And who I am is a bundle of paradoxes and contradictions: I believe and I doubt, I trust and I get discouraged, I love and I hate, I feel bad about feeling good, I feel guilty if I don't feel guilty. Aristotle said we are rational animals. I say I am an angel with an incredible capacity for beer. It is the real me that God loves. I don't have to be anyone else. For 20 years I tried to be Brother Teresa. I tried to be Francis of Assisi. I had to be a carbon copy of a great saint rather than the original God intended me to be. The biggest mistake I can make is to say to God, "Lord, if I change, you'll love me, won't you?" The Lord's reply is always, "Wait a minute, you've got it all wrong. You don't have to change so I'll love you; I love you so you'll change." I simply expose myself to the love that is everything and have an immense, unshakable, reckless, raging confidence that God loves me so much he'll change me and fashion me into the child that he always wanted me to be.

"Faith is the courage to accept acceptance," says Paul Tillich. At the heart of real faith is a deep conviction that God knows us and loves us as we are and not as we should be. Furthermore, we can love God and move toward obedience to Him because He first loved us. God's love compels us, says Paul (2 Corinthians 5:14).

He guides me in paths of righteousness . . .

> *Oh that my baa-ing nature would win hence*
> *   Some woolly innocence!*
>
> —C. S. LEWIS

"If I don't have the hope of one day being good," a friend once confided in me, "if there is no escape from the evil I keep doing, nothing could reconcile me to life." I share his sentiment.

God does too: He would have us

rid of all discontent, all fear, all grudging,
all bitterness in word or thought, all gaug-
ing and measuring of ourselves with a different rod from that we would apply to
another. He would have no curling of the
lip; no indifference in us to the man whose
service in any form we use; no desire to
excel another, no contentment at gaining
by his loss. He would not have us receive
the smallest service without gratitude;
would not hear from us a tone to jar the
heart of another, a word to make it ache, be
the ache ever so transient.

—GEORGE MACDONALD

It is God's will that we should be holy
(1 Thessalonians 4:3), by which Paul assures us
that God's ultimate intent is to make us good.
Every day He is leading us along the path toward
righteousness.

We're inclined to think of God's will solely in
terms of where we will go and what we will do when
we get there, and certainly God does have a plan
for each moment of our lives. But God's direction

primarily has to do with holiness and His determination to change us beyond recognition—to make us as good as He is.

The goodness that comes from God

Some people try too hard; they're upright, but uptight. Goodness, for them, is stern, demanding business. They're chaste, honest, sober, respectable, Bible-toting, church-going, psalm-singing people, but everything seems out of phase. As William James said, "Their faith exists as a 'dull habit.'" They have an appearance of righteousness with their self-imposed worship, obvious humility, and harsh treatment of the body, but they lack the cordial love that springs from contact with God.

Edicts, dictums, creeds, rites, rituals can never modify us; nor do admonitions to read the Bible more, pray more, and go to church more often. There is a life beyond earnestness. "From such silly devotions deliver us, good Lord," prayed St. Francis of Avila.

The problem with rules and regulations is that they have no mechanism for overriding our natural tendencies to go wrong. All they can do is reveal those tendencies and say to us, "You should!" "You shouldn't!" "You haven't!" "You can't!" The rest is up to us.

It takes too much energy to keep the rules. We must never lose control. We must maintain a safe distance from people and resist intimacy. But though the spirit may be willing the flesh is weak. Inevitably we get weary and sick of trying. Then, no matter how hard we try to suppress our instincts, we become unable to sustain the effort. Some unsightly, emotional display, some inappropriate reaction to a relational failure, some other humiliating behavior blows our cover. Our facade cracks and others see behind it. We have that horrible experience of being found out. Others come to know what we have known all along—that much of us is ugly and unacceptable.

No, self-effort doesn't work. It only makes things worse. We must take sin seriously and want with all of our hearts to put it away, but we must not be self-conscious, compulsive, and preoccupied about it. As a plaque on a friend's wall reads, "Today I will not should on myself."

> *Suffer us not to mock ourselves with falsehood*
> *Teach us to care and not to care*
> *Teach us to sit still*

Even among these rocks
Our peace in His will . . .
And let my cry come unto Thee.

—T. S. ELIOT

A job for God . . .

Goodness is a job for God. We must stop horning in on His business and instead ask Him to bring about our change: To those "who are far from righteousness," He says, "I am *bringing* my righteousness near" (Isaiah 46:12–13).

Being godly does require discipline, but that discipline should never be construed as a rigorous technique. Following Christ requires effort, but it is the effort to stay close to Him and listen to His voice. Serious effort is needed if we are to focus on Him and become sensitive to His desires.

As we draw close to Him—walking with Him, talking to Him, listening to His words, relying on Him, asking for His help—His character begins to rub off on us. Quietly and unobtrusively His influence softens our wills, making us thirsty for righteousness, inclining us to do His pleasure, restraining our passions, keeping us from evil, making us ashamed of evil, giving us the courage to choose what is good. In His quiet love He takes all that's unworthy in us and gradually turns it into something worthwhile for Him.

Change is not passive; we must hate evil and love righteousness. To love righteousness is to will it to grow. It's a matter of inclination and desire. It's not what we are, but what we *want* to be that matters. Do we want righteousness? Do we want to do better? "When the fight begins within himself, a man's worth something," Robert Browning said.

Paul puts it this way: "The one who sows to please his sinful nature, from that nature will reap destruction; the one who sows to please the Spirit, from the Spirit will reap eternal life. Let us not become weary in doing good, for at the proper time we will reap a harvest if we do not give up" (Galatians 6:8–9). It's the law: Every time we sow to the flesh—harbor a grudge, nurse a grievance, wallow in self-interest and self-pity—we are sowing seeds of self-destruction. On the other hand, every time we till the soil of the Spirit—long to please God's Spirit and ask for His help—we sow seeds that will endure to eternal life. Every time we make a right choice, God begins to turn us into someone a little different from the person we were before.

We cannot rid ourselves of our sins, "but we can set about sending them away. We can quarrel with them and proceed to turn them out. The Lord is on his way to do his part in their final banishment" (George MacDonald). God is the only source of authentic and lasting change. Whatever conformity to goodness we achieve is the fruit of His doing.

Fruit is exactly the right word, suggesting as it does some hidden element, quietly at work to produce results. Jesus said: "I am the vine; you are the branches. If a man remains in me and I in him, he will bear much fruit; apart from me you can do nothing" (John 15:5). The relationship of a branch to its vine is the relationship we must sustain to our Lord: We must remain, or *abide*, to use the older term. We must set aside everything we normally rely on and cling to Him—closely joined to Him, sustained by His life, waiting for His impulses that will in time produce the fruit of righteousness for which we yearn.

"There is no true virtue without a miracle," Augustine said. God must work His magic on us. Any progress we make toward righteousness is the product of our association with Him. We must come again and again to Him with our desires and lofty ideals and lay them at His feet. We must bring our weakness, our shame, our compulsions, our doubts and fears, our misjudgments, our weariness, and our staleness and ask Him to complete us. He is the only one who can take the vision of all that we have never been and bring it into being.

Waiting . . .

Waiting is a necessary part of the process. There are no shortcuts to maturity. Our personalities resist change, flawed as they are by nature, nurture, and our own indulgence. We've been wounded by others and we've wounded ourselves, yet we can be assured that our healing is going on every day. We are in recovery, gradually being delivered from evil. God is working even now for that distant end. We are becoming today what we will inevitably be. We must

> *Wait for God's silent molding;*
> *Wait for his full unfolding;*
> *Wait for the days to be.*
> —FRANCES HAVERGAL

We must believe that God's processes are adequate to deal with our sin. The key word is *process.* We must "be comfortable with ourselves in process," as a friend of mine once said. God heals by degrees. We grow slowly from one degree of likeness to the next—inch by inch, here a little, there a little. "We, who with unveiled faces all reflect the Lord's glory, are being transformed into his likeness with ever-increasing glory, which comes from the Lord, who is the Spirit" (2 Corinthians 3:18). Gain is gain, however small.

When God wants to change us we will know; we will feel what Danish philosopher Sören Kierkegaard called "the infinite weight of God." The sign of God's convicting is never free-floating guilt and a vague sense of wrong. That's the devil's doing. When God speaks to us there is little ground for doubt or confusion. We are unmistakably convinced of our sin. When that convincing comes we can turn to Him from our sin—*repent,* to use the biblical word—thank Him for His forgiveness, and ask for His enabling. Then we can leave the process to Him and go on.

And going on is all that matters. God doesn't look for perfection, only progress. We're certain of failing, but not overcome with fear. "Nothing will undo us if we keep picking ourselves up each time.

We shall of course be very muddy and tattered children by the time we reach home. . . . The only fatal thing is to lose one's temper and give up" (C. S. Lewis).

As for me, if I've made any progress at all, it's not been by quantum leaps and bounds, but by tentative steps and a number of falls. It's been a creeping thing, better seen in retrospect than in prospect. The path has been chaotic and haphazard, but I have David's confidence: God is leading me in paths of righteousness. Every day He is taking me along the path toward the place He wants me to be.

Everything worthwhile takes time, but time is on our side. We have the rest of our lives to grow. God is wonderfully patient. He will never give up on us until His work is done. What He is making of you and me is not yet complete—we are unfinished—but one day very soon God will finish. "Dear friends, now we are children of God," John assures us, "and what we will be has not yet been made known. But we know that when he appears, we shall be like him" (1 John 3:2).

And that's good enough for me.

EVEN THOUGH I WALK THROUGH THE VALLEY OF THE SHADOW OF DEATH, I WILL FEAR NO EVIL, FOR YOU ARE WITH ME; YOUR ROD AND YOUR STAFF, THEY COMFORT ME

In pastures green? Not always; sometimes He
Who knoweth best, in kindness leadeth me
In weary ways, where heavy shadows be.

—H. H. BARRY

IN THE MIDDLE OF THE MEADOW the path plunges down into the valley of the shadow of death. The words awaken primal memories and stir up ominous images. In all of Scripture there's no place more familiar than this and none more evocative.

101

I remember the impression I had as a child when I first heard the words, "the valley of the shadow of death." I conjured up a mental picture of a storm-shrouded landscape, a yawning abyss at my feet, broken crags, precipitous cliffs, and a narrow, twisting footpath along narrow ledges, leading inexorably into thickening gloom below. The picture is locked in my mind.

The phrase *shadow of death* is one word in Hebrew, meaning "deep darkness." It's a dreary word, used elsewhere in the Bible to describe the impenetrable darkness before creation (Amos 5:8), the thick darkness of a mine shaft (Job 28:3), and the black hole that is the abode of the dead (Job 10:21; 38:17). It's a word associated with anxiety and unfocused dread.

In *The Pilgrim's Progress* John Bunyan captures something of the terror of the place when he describes it as "dark as pitch," inhabited by "hobgoblins, satyrs, dragons of the pit and fiends." A way "set full of pits, pitfalls, deep holes and shelvings." In the midst of the valley was "the mouth of hell."

As Bunyan's pilgrim and his companion ventured into the valley they saw that "there was on the right hand a very deep ditch. . . . Again, behold on the left hand, there was a very dangerous quag, into which, if even a good man falls, he can find no bottom for his foot to stand on. Into that quag King David did fall, and had no doubt therein been smothered, had not He that is able, plucked him out."

The valley of the shadow of death is usually associated with the end of life, but Bunyan places it in the middle, where it rightly belongs. In fact there is not one valley; there are many, falling between the pastures where we find intermittent rest. There's no way around them. "We *must* go through many hardships to enter the kingdom of God," Paul insists (Acts 14:22). The desolate places are an inevitable and necessary part of the journey.

The valleys bring to mind the day an employer said "clean out your desk"; when a doctor said "your baby will never be normal"; when you found the stash in your son's closet; when your teenage daughter told you she was pregnant; when the doctor said you had cancer; when your spouse said he or she had no energy left to put into the relationship.

Those are the dark days when we lose all perspective, when we say in despair, "It's no use; I can't go on."

The valleys are emblematic of periods of prolonged failure when we're shamed and broken by the full weight of the darkness within us; when we

experience the isolation of despair, the exhausted
aftermath of self-gratification and spent vice; when
we feel unalterably defiled and wonder if we will
ever regain our sense of worth.

The valleys symbolize those dreary days of
deep loneliness when we say with David, "No one
is concerned for me. I have no refuge; no one cares
for my life" (Psalm 142:4); when no one seeks us;
no one asks about us; there are no cards or letters;
the phone doesn't ring; no one seems to care. Even
God seems aloof and remote; there's an unaccount-
able chill in the air. We cry out with David, "My
God, my God, why have you forsaken me? Why
are you so far from saving me, so far from the
words of my groaning? O my God, I cry out by
day, but you do not answer" (Psalm 22:1–2).

Oh, yes, there are valleys far worse than
death.

Suffering successfully

I used to think that life was mostly green pasture with an occasional dark valley along the way,
but now I realize it's the other way around. There
are days of surprising joy, but much of life is a vale
of tears.

Life is difficult. "The world is painful in any case; but it is quite unbearable if anybody gives us the idea that we are meant to be liking it," Charles Williams said.

When people tell me that life is hard, I reply, "Of course it is." I find that answer more satisfying than anything else I can say. Every year confirms my belief that life is indeed difficult and demanding. Any other view of life is escapist.

The path by which God takes us often seems to lead away from our good, causing us to believe we've missed a turn and taken the wrong road. That's because most of us have been taught to believe that if we're on the right track God's goodness will always translate into earthly good: that He'll heal, deliver, and exempt us from disease and pain; that we'll have money in the bank, kids who turn out well, nice clothes, a comfortable living, and a leisurely retirement. In that version of life everyone turns out to be a winner, nobody loses a business, fails in marriage, or lives in poverty.

But that's a pipe dream far removed from the biblical perspective that God's love often leads us down roads where earthly comforts fail us so He can give us eternal consolation (2 Thessalonians 2:16). "Suffering ripens our souls," said Alexander Solzhenitsyn.

God doesn't cushion the journey; He lets life jolt us. We should keep that idea in mind when the way seems difficult and long. As F. B. Meyer said, if we've been told that we're supposed to be on a bumpy track, every jolt along the way simply confirms the fact that we're still on the right road.

When we come to the end of all valleys we'll understand that every path has been selected, out of all possible options, for our ultimate good. God, in fact, could not have taken us by any other way. No other route would have been as safe and as certain as the one by which we came. And if only we could see the path as God has always seen it, we would select it as well.

He chose this path for me,
Though well he knew that thorns would pierce my feet,
Knew how the brambles would obstruct the way,
Knew all the hidden dangers I would meet,
Knew how my faith would falter day by day;
And still my whisper echoes, "Yes I see
This path is best for me."

He chose this path for me;
Why need I more: this better truth to know,
That all along these strange bewildering ways,

O'er rocky steeps where dark rivers flow,
  His mighty arm will bear me all my days
    A few steps more, and I shall see
    This path is best for me.

—J. R. MILLER

You are with me . . .

When Bunyan's pilgrim plunged into the valley he heard the voice of a man going before him, saying, "Even though I walk through the valley of the shadow of death, I will fear no evil, for *you* are with me." He gathered that others were in the valley as well, and that God was with them. "Why not with me?" he gathered, "though by reason of the impediment that attends this place, I cannot perceive it."

That was David's conclusion: "Even though I walk through the valley of the shadow of death, I will fear no evil for *you are with me.* Your rod and your staff, they comfort me." His Shepherd was by his side, armed to the teeth, warding off his enemies and keeping him from wandering off the trail. God was with him in the midst of his fears.

The grammar of this poem shifts significantly at this point. David moves from speaking of God in the third person, he, to the second person, you. He had been speaking *about* God; in the valley he turns and speaks *to* Him. That's a small detail in the text, but it makes a big difference to our hearts to know that God is with us in the valley. His presence was David's comfort.

What God said to Moses is true for all times: "My Presence will go with you, and I will give you rest" (Exodus 33:14). He said to Jacob: "*I am with you* and will watch over you wherever you go" (Genesis 28:15). He said to Joshua: "As I was with Moses, so *I will be with you*; I will never leave you nor forsake you" (Joshua 1:5). He said to Israel: "Do not fear, for *I am with you*; do not be dismayed, for I am your God. I will strengthen you and help you; I will uphold you with my righteous right hand. . . . When you pass through the waters, *I will be with you;* and when you pass through the rivers, they will not sweep over you. When you walk through the fire, you will not be burned; the flames will not set you ablaze" (Isaiah 41:10; 43:2). He says to us: "Surely *I am with you always*, to the very end of the age" (Matthew 28:20).

God is with us, walking everywhere incognito, as C. S. Lewis said. "And the incognito is not always hard to penetrate. The real labor is to remember, to

108

attend. In fact, to come awake. Still more, to remain awake." The main thing to remember is to make ourselves think about His presence; to acknowledge that He is with us, as real as He was in the days of His flesh when He walked with His disciples amid the sorrows and haunts of this world.

Friends fail us, spouses walk out on us, parents disappoint us, therapists refuse to return our calls, but God is with us every moment of every day. When we ford the deep waters, when we pass through the fire, when we walk through the valley of the shadow of death, He is there.

Difficulty and drudgery make us think of ourselves as being all alone, but He has said, "I will never leave you nor forsake you." Of Him alone it can be said, He will never say good-bye.

About, above me, evermore
God's gentle presence broods,
He shares with me my silences,
He fills my solitudes.

His face and form I cannot see,
No spoken word can hear,
But with some better sense of soul
Do I perceive him near.

Are not these joys too good to last?
May he not soon depart?
'No, I am with you all the days'
He answers to my heart.

—UNKNOWN

Seeing what cannot be seen . . .

"God becomes a reality," Richard Foster says, "when he becomes a necessity." The dark valleys make God more real to us than ever before. How many times have I heard from those who have endured intense suffering that the experience of their pain has cured them of the idolatries that once robbed them of joy. The father who abandons us, the spouse who leaves us, the financial catastrophe that ruins us, the rude interruption of our plans, the revelation of a horrifying illness, the painful, pro- longed delay—all escalate our love for God. All are His ways of prying our fingers from things that are false and that will not satisfy. They pull us away from lesser loves and enlarge our intimacy with our Shepherd, which is what brings us peace and unimaginable joy.

"One sees the truth more clearly when one is unhappy," wrote Fyodor Dostoevsky from Siberia.

Then he continued:

> And yet God gives me moments of perfect
> peace; in such moments I love and believe
> that I am loved; in such moments I have
> formulated my creed, wherein all is clear
> and holy to me. This creed is extremely
> simple: here it is. I believe that there is
> nothing lovelier, deeper, more sympathetic,
> more rational, more manly and more per-
> fect than the Savior: I say to myself with
> jealous love that not only is there no one
> else like him, but that there could be no
> one.

We're inclined to fix on the valley and its
pain, but God chooses to look forward and antici-
pate its effect. He deals with our divided hearts
through disappointment, grief, and tears, weaning
us from other loves and passions and centering us
on Him. We learn to trust Him in the darkness;
when all that is left is the sound of His voice and
the knowledge that He is near; when all we can do
is slip our hand into His and feel "the familiar clasp
of things divine." These are times that wean us
away from sensuality—that tendency to live by feel-
ings rather than by faith in God's unseen presence.

We become independent of places and moods and content with God alone.

The dark days cause us to enter into a very special relationship with our Lord. As Job said, "My ears had heard of you, but now my eyes have seen you" (Job 42:5). There are glimpses of God that can only be revealed when earthly joy has ceased.

The most perfect human love cannot satisfy us. That's because our human hearts crave for a relationship deeper and more lasting than anything possible in this world. We were made for God's love and without it we sink into loneliness. The darkness, the breakdown of human ties, the limitations and losses of human affection lead to that higher friendship, that larger, more permanent love.

> *God's strong arm*
> *extends to selfish bullies, willful, crude;*
> *endures the self-deceived; ignores the rude;*
> *forbears with murder; incest does not quell—*
> *and when my arm would sweep them all to hell,*
> *He draws them to his heart.*

> *God's strong arm*
> *in love applies the rod, employs the lash;*
> *impairs a face; in beauty strikes a gash;*
> *denies the hungry; wounds a mother's breast.*

And while I raise my fist, beseech, protest,
He draws me to his heart.

—RUTH BELL GRAHAM

David himself understood the adversity that draws us to God's heart. Subjected to neglect by his mother and father and demeaned by the rest of his family, he was deeply scarred. His family would have ruined him if he had not fled to his heavenly Father for refuge. Out of his loneliness and heartache David wrote, "Though my father and mother have forsaken me, the LORD has taken me in" (Psalm 27:10).

And then the work went on . . .

> *Latest born of Jesse's race,*
> > *wonder lights thy bashful face,*
> *While the prophet's gifted oil,*
> > *seals thee for a life of toil.*
> *Heartache, woeful care, distress,*
> > *blighted hope, and loneliness;*
> *Wounds from friend and gifts from foe,*
> > *dizzied faith, and guilt, and woe;*
> *Loftiest aims by earth defiled,*
> > *gleams of wisdom sin-beguiled;*

> *Sated power's tyrranic mood,*
> *counsels shared by men of blood;*
> *Sad success, parental tears,*
> *and a dreary gift of years.*

—UNKNOWN

David was hammered and hurt throughout his entire life, every blow converting him, exposing his ambivalence, until he would finally cry, "Surely, I was sinful at birth, sinful from the time my mother conceived me. . . . Create in me a pure [undivided] heart" (Psalm 51:5, 10).

God's work is never done: "Thus always—the rod, the stripes, the chastisements; but amid all, the love of God, carrying out his redemptive purpose, never hasting, never resting, never forgetting, but making all things work together until the evil is eliminated and the soul is purified" (F. B. Meyer).

Then David cried out, "My soul finds rest in God *alone* . . ." (Psalm 62:1). It was through darkness, suffering, and pain that all David's passions were integrated into one.

And so, all of life is consummated in loving God. That's what we were made for; that's where ultimate satisfaction lies. If that's true, and I firmly believe it is, then although it is often hard to do, we should welcome any valley that leads us to Him.

There will be an end . . .

One thing more: No valley goes on forever. We walk *through* the valley of the shadow of death. God knows what we can endure. He will not let us be tempted or tested beyond what we can bear (1 Corinthians 10:13). The deliverance we seek may be subject to delay, but we must never doubt that our day will come. "Weeping may remain for a night, but rejoicing comes in the morning" (Psalm 30:5). Sorrow has its time to be, but God will mitigate the tears when their work is done. Those who mourn will be comforted. There will be an end.

YOU PREPARE A TABLE BEFORE ME IN THE PRESENCE OF MY ENEMIES. YOU ANOINT MY HEAD WITH OIL; MY CUP OVERFLOWS

*"Hush! What if this friend
happens to be—God!"*

—ELIZABETH BARRETT BROWNING

SOME SAY THAT DAVID DROPPED THE SHEPHERD FIGURE at this point and shifted to another metaphor, but I see no need to cut the poem in two. The scene is still pastoral: The first four verses portray the shepherd with his sheep in the pasture; the final two verses place him in his tent providing sanctuary, serving as a gracious host, spreading a lavish meal, overwhelming his guests with hospitality.

The ancient shepherd's tent was a safe house where "every wanderer, whatever his character, or his past might be, was received as a 'guest of God'—such is the beautiful name they still give him—furnished with food, and kept inviolable, his host becoming responsible for his safety" (George Adam Smith).

It was this custom that David had in mind when he composed this line.

We are God's guests! He seats us at His table; He welcomes all comers. It's not as though He doesn't know what we're like. We're uninteresting, exasperating, and otherwise unattractive company, but there's no censure or condescension, only eternal affirmation and supply. He welcomes us warmly and overwhelms us with His lavish love.

> *Love bade me welcome; yet my soul drew back*
> *   Guilty of dust and sin.*
> *But quick-eyed Love, observing me grow slack*
> *   From my first entrance in,*
> *Drew nearer to me, sweetly questioning*
> *   If I lacked anything.*
> *"A guest," I answered, "worthy to be here."*
> *   Love said, "You shall be he."*

"I the kind, the ungrateful? Ah, my dear,
    I cannot look on thee."
Love took my hand, and smiling did reply,
    "Who made the eyes but I?"
"Truth, Lord, but I have marred them: let my shame
    Go where it doth deserve."
"And know you not," says Love, "who bore the
blame?"
    "My dear, then I will serve."
"You must sit down," says Love, "and taste my
meat,"
    So I did sit and eat.

—GEORGE HERBERT

It is God's nature to humble Himself and
serve. Think of the occasion when Jesus gathered
His disciples in the upper room.

Jesus knew that the time had come for him
to leave this world and go to the Father.
Having loved his own who were in the
world, he now showed them the full extent
of his love. . . . He got up from the meal,
took off his outer clothing, and wrapped a
towel around his waist. After that, he
poured water into a basin and began to

wash his disciples' feet, drying them with
the towel that was wrapped around him.

—JOHN 13:1, 4–5

Footwashing was an essential act of hospitality
in those days. Normally servants performed that
unbecoming task, but there were no servants in the
apostolic band and no one volunteered for the job.
So our Lord took on the duty. Girding Himself as a
servant, He stooped and washed His disciples' feet,
one by one.

We never think much about the humility of
God. Theologians remark on His other attributes
but rarely on that virtue. Imagine: the Incarnate God
of the universe, garbed as a servant, girded with a
towel, on hands and knees washing rank and filthy
feet, moving steadily downward in submission and
service to those in need—even to Judas who was
about to betray Him. What incredible modesty!

There was also the time when our Lord fed
His disciples beside the Sea of Galilee. They had
been fishing all night but had caught nothing. They
were tired, dispirited, gloomy. "When they landed,
they saw a fire of burning coals there with fish on
it, and some bread. . . . Jesus said to them, 'Come
and have breakfast' " (John 21:9, 12).

John says the disciples *knew* it was the Lord. They recognized Him by that propensity to cater to others; always, there was His inclination to serve. He came not to be ministered to, but to minister—to us.

To such a one we come. He delights to serve. His giving supplies the nourishment our spirits crave. At His table there is "wine that gladdens the heart of man, oil to make his face shine, and bread that sustains his heart" (Psalm 104:15). He gives full measure, pressed down, running over. His grace is more than sufficient; His goodness over-flows; we have all and abound!

"You anoint my head with oil," David says. Anointing the head with oil was a token of esteem in ancient times. Love was manifest by the costliness of the oils. Myrrh, aloes, cassia, and other exotic fra-grances were mixed together in precise measure and permanently sealed in alabaster vases. When the time came for anointing one's guests, the bottles were broken at the neck and the oil inside was poured lavishly onto the heads of the guests until it ran down onto the person's robes, leaving a lingering fragrance. It was called the "oil of joy" (Psalm 45:7).

"My cup overflows," David continues. He sees God hovering over him, waiting for the moment of slightest need, filling and refilling his cup with wine. David has more than enough. "Abundance and redundance are his," as one old saint said.

> Does David not mean us to infer that life is a feast, in which we are guests and God is the host? And does he not also mean to teach that God greets us in love and welcome?—He is not niggardly or churlish, but glad to see us glad and to make us happy; conferring on us luxuries as well as necessities; and taking pains at great cost to Himself, to show us that he is well pleased to accept us and show us grace in the Beloved.
>
> —F. B. MEYER

God's table is a metaphor for His gracious, ongoing provision. "Can God spread a table in the desert?" we ask (Psalm 78:19). Can He meet our needs in the midst of our dearth? You bet your life He can! God is able to supply *all* our needs; He is equal to all our emergencies and essential needs.

God wants to give. Ask and receive, Jesus said. That's the utter simplicity of faith. For all our desire He gives all of Himself. All that He is, is ours.

When we understand the fullness of His heart and His desire to give we can ask anything. That vision of God "makes life a continuous prayer," said Bishop Walcott.

We should understand that God's resources are granted neither for shows of strength nor for selfish ambition. God has a greater thing in mind for us: Most of His giving is to make us good.

Jesus put it this way: "I am the vine; you are the branches. If a man remains in me and I in him, he will bear much fruit; apart from me you can do nothing. . . . *If you remain in me and my words remain in you, ask whatever you wish, and it will be given you.* This is to my Father's glory, that you bear much fruit, showing yourselves to be my disciples" (John 15:5, 7–8). His unequivocal promise: "Ask whatever you wish and it will be given you," is conditioned by the context and controlled by the concept of fruit. The "fruit" is the fruit of the Spirit: "love, joy, peace, patience, kindness, goodness, faithfulness, gentleness and self-control" (Galatians 5:22).

We can ask anything that involves acquiring the characteristics of God. When we ask for His character He begins to give it, working through time and circumstance to conform us more closely to His will. This is the use to which He puts His power.

When we've come to the end of our resources, when we've run out of all that's essential—that's when God comes through.

"Heaven helps those that help themselves," is supposed to be ancient wisdom, but it's not something you'd ever hear God say. It sounds more like good advice from the devil. God insists that heaven helps those who are helpless. King Uzziah of Judah was "greatly helped *until* he became powerful" according to the prophet (2 Chronicles 26:15). Uzziah's strength was his failing; it tied God's hands. When the king got too powerful God couldn't help him any more.

"I yam what I yam," Popeye says. By the grace of God, we are what we are, and what we are is inadequate. Inadequacy is a fact of life, a hard truth that makes life much easier when we accept it. "We're all ordinary people," G. K. Chesterton said, "and it's the *extra*ordinary people who know it."

The problem with us is that we're much too well equipped and much too adept at what we do. We believe too much in ourselves—in our experience, our education, our appearance, our humor, our personality. But our essential humanity is useless. "The flesh [human effort] counts for nothing" (John 6:63).

"Blessed are the poor," Jesus said. By *poor* He meant "poverty-stricken," a word commonly used in the Gospels for beggars who sat on the streets in rags and in utter need, holding out their hands, appealing to others for aid. These are the people who catch God's eye. "This is the one I esteem: he who is humble [poor] and contrite in spirit, and trembles at my word" (Isaiah 66:2).

Human limitation is a fact of life. It's foolish to believe that we're strong. It doesn't take much to bring us down: a tiny virus can devastate us physically, a slight miscalculation can ruin us financially, a small miscue can undo us socially. Life cannot be controlled and contained; there are just too many contingencies. We don't have what it takes.

Howard Butt, in an article entitled "The Art of Being the Big Shot," said this:

> It is my pride that makes me think I call
> my own shots. That feeling is my basic dis-
> honesty. I can't go it alone. I can't rely on
> myself. I am dependent on God for my
> very next breath. It is dishonest of me to
> pretend that I am anything but a man,
> small, weak, limited. So living independent
> of God is self-delusion. It is not just a matter

of pride being an unfortunate little trait and humility being an attractive little virtue. It is my inner psychological integrity that is at stake. When I am self-dependent, I am lying to myself about what I am. I am pretending to be God and not man. My independence is the idolatrous worship of myself, the national religion of hell.

Some people asked Jesus once what good work God required. Jesus' answer caught them completely by surprise: "The work of God is this: to *believe* in the one he has sent" (John 6:28–29). How audacious of anyone to think that mere human beings can do God's work. If anything is to be done at all He must do it.

Whatever we have to do—putting down the smallest rising thought of anger and wrong or selfishness in our souls, giving up our hard-earned leisure time to serve someone in need, showing quiet, unnoticed compassion to another—it must be done by faith. Those who work the works of God are those who realize their unfitness and utter inadequacy and rely on Him for His strength.

We are flimsy and frail—"thinking reeds," Pascal said. Easily crushed and bruised. The world overwhelms us. We wear out; we become weary and worn thin. The tragedies and ambiguities of life sap our strength and bring us to our knees. "Even youths grow tired and weary, and the young men stumble and fall" (Isaiah 40:30). We are limited, dependent beings, but therein lies our strength. When we are weak, says Paul, then we are strong (2 Corinthians 12:10).

> *Crushed!—it filled with patience,*
> *Wounded!—it beamed with love,*
> *Wearied!—it mounted upward,*
> *Up to a great life above.*
>
> *Weak!—it grew with greatness,*
> *Feeble!—it rose with strength,*
> *Fitful!—it heaved majestic,*
> *Heaved to calm peace at length.*
>
> *This is the constitution,*
> *Opposites always combined,*
> *Of body, soul, and spirit,*
> *Limited—undefined.*
>
> —OSWALD CHAMBERS

Isaiah insists that those who hope in the Lord will exchange their strength for God's. "They will soar on wings like eagles; they will run and not grow weary, they will walk and not faint" (Isaiah 40:31).

Our limits are limitless, but He has no limits. No demand is too difficult, no dilemma too hard, no complication too complicated. He never wears out, gets weary, or grows tired. When we acknowledge our boundaries and ask for His help, He replaces our "strength" with His.

Some days we outdo the eagles and rise above our circumstances, unconfined and unencumbered; we soar and see things from God's point of view. (Enjoy such moments!)

There are other days when, as the White Queen said to Alice, "it takes all the running you can to keep in the same place," or in the words of a plaque that used to hang over my mother's desk, the "hurrier you go the behinder you get." Those are the days we can maintain the pace with poise and persistence, sustained by God's inexhaustible strength.

And then there are those ordinary days when the desk is piled with dreary duties or the sink is full of dirty dishes and the routine is tedious and dull; when, as Ruth Bell Graham recalled, there's only "nothingness, inertia, skies gray and windless, no sun, no rain, no stab of pain, no strong regret, no reaching after, no tears, no laughter, no black despair, no bliss."

God delivers us through this. We can walk when the novelty has worn off, when the glory has faded, when the strength of youth is gone. This is the strength of God.

God's boundless, uninterrupted strength freely exchanged for our merely human effort? God's greatness flowing through our basic incompetence? This is grace!

> *When we have exhausted our store of endurance,*
> *When our strength has failed ere the day is*
> *half done,*
> *When we reach the end of our hoarded resources,*
> *Our Father's full giving is only begun.*
> *His love has no limit, His grace has no measure*
> *His power no boundary known unto men;*
> *For out of his infinite riches in Jesus*
> *He giveth and giveth and giveth again.*
>
> —ANNIE JOHNSON FLINT

There's something winsome and wonderfully compelling about those whom God is making strong. They're easier to get along with, easier to work with and live with, more gentle and genial. Their goodness is like old wine—mellow and fragrant. They have a profound and bewildering effect upon others. Their actions keep reminding people of . . . well, of God.

That sort of influence cannot be conjured up or contrived. It's not a matter of feminine force or male machismo; it's not a function of self-assertiveness, intellect, charisma, charm, or chutzpah. It *happens*— the fruit of our association with God.

Self-conscious influence is pretentious and puts people off. It looks like what it is: *self*-righteousness, and it annoys others to no end. When we try to be influential we become aggressive and intrusive. We crowd people and push them away from the truth. (When we do so, we're sure of just one ally—the devil.) But those whom God is making good are powerfully persuasive. They have a fragrance like a subtle perfume. Wherever they go, they leave behind the unforgettable aroma of their Lord (2 Corinthians 2:14–17).

God is never done. His work of nourishing us and strengthening us goes on all through our lives. Paul writes, "We do not lose heart. Though outwardly we are wasting away, yet inwardly we are being renewed day by day (2 Corinthians 4:16).

As age breaks down our natural energy and strength we're more inclined than ever before to depend on God's provision. We have more time for contemplation and prayer. His nearness keeps rubbing off on us. We reflect more of His goodness. Youthful knowledge and zeal, tempered by worship and God-awareness, become the wisdom that time alone can yield. What once we did with youthful strength we now can do with greater sensitivity and humbler hearts. Wisdom softens our faces.

Then our influence has a peculiar power. Tested character and ripened experience has a spiritual vitality and vision that a busier age cannot have. Those at the beginning of life acquire knowledge, but those more near its end gain gentle wisdom. It has to do with character and people skills and kinder, gentler ways of getting things done. That wisdom is "pure; then peace-loving, considerate, submissive, full of mercy and good fruit, impartial and sincere" (James 3:17).

We grow to ceilings in every other realm of life, but there are no ceilings to growth in grace. No one yet has ever outgrown God's willingness to give. As our days, so shall our strength be.

> *Give me strength for my day, Lord,*
> *That wheresoe'er I go,*

There shall no danger daunt me
*   And I shall fear no foe;*
So shall no task o'ercome me,
*   So shall no trial fret,*
So shall I walk unwearied
*   The path where my feet are set;*
So shall I find no burden
*   Greater than I can bear,*
So shall I have a courage
*   Equal to all my care;*
So shall no grief o'erwhelm me,
*   So shall no wave o'erflow;*
Give me Thy strength for my day, Lord,
*   Cover my weakness so.*

—ANNIE JOHNSON FLINT

SURELY GOODNESS AND LOVE WILL FOLLOW ME ALL THE DAYS OF MY LIFE, AND I WILL DWELL IN THE HOUSE OF THE LORD FOREVER.

Abashed the devil stood and felt how awful goodness is.

—JOHN MILTON

"SURELY GOODNESS AND LOVE WILL FOLLOW ME all the days of my life," David declares. "Surely," denotes a fact as certain as it is comforting. Too good to be true? No, God is much too good not to be true.

He is *good*—as good as we're capable of imagining Him to be—the only good person in the world. As Jesus said with such utter finality, *"No one* is good—except God" (Luke 18:19).

133

He is *love*—as loving as we need Him to be. Everything is about love—or the lack of it, as reductionists say. It's a simple human fact that we cannot long survive without tenderness, caring, and someone who is willing to accept us as we are.

The psalms are filled with affirmations of God's love for us: "I trust in your unfailing *love*" (13:5), David writes. "I . . . rejoice in your *love*" (31:7). "You are forgiving and good, O Lord, abounding in *love* to all who call to you" (86:5). "The LORD is good and his *love* endures forever" (100:5). "Give thanks to the LORD, for he is good; his *love* endures forever" (106—2 times). "Give thanks to the LORD, for he is good; his *love* endures forever" (Psalm 118—5 times). "Give thanks to the LORD, for he is good; his *love* endures forever" (Psalm 136—26 times).

David's word for God's tender affection is a term used in the ancient world to mean love that flows out of deep emotion rather than duty. It's a kind and gentle love. That quaint, old word *lovingkindness* may still be the best translation of all.

It's the way God thinks of Himself: "The LORD, the LORD, the compassionate and gracious God, slow to anger, abounding in [*lovingkindness*] and faithfulness" (Exodus 34:6). David took that revelation to heart, twice quoting God's exact words: "But you, O Lord, are a compassionate and gracious God, slow to anger, abounding in [*lovingkindness*] and faithfulness (Psalms 86:15; see 103:8).

David often linked God's goodness and lovingkindness together. In his mind they were inseparable components of God's gracious care. Here in his shepherd poem he personifies these two attributes as God Himself. In these tender manifestations He follows us, shadowing us, attending us, assuring us that no matter what transpires today, tomorrow, or the next day—it cannot separate us from God's goodness and love.

"Who shall separate us from the love of Christ?" says Paul.

> Shall trouble or hardship or persecution or famine or nakedness or danger or sword? As it is written: "For your sake we face death all day long; we are considered as sheep to be slaughtered." No, in all these things we are more than conquerors through him who loved us. For I am convinced that neither death nor life, neither angels nor demons, neither the present nor the future, nor any powers, neither height nor depth, nor any-

thing else in all creation, will be able to separate us from the love of God that is in Christ Jesus our Lord.

—ROMANS 8:35–37

I may fall flat on my face; I may fail until I feel old and beaten and done in. Yet your goodness and love is changeless. All the music may go out of my life, my private world may shatter to dust. Even so, you hold me in the palm of your steady hand. No turn in the affairs of my fractured life can baffle you. Satan with all his braggadocio cannot distract you. Nothing can separate me from your measureless love—pain can't, disappointment can't, anguish can't. Yesterday, today, tomorrow can't. The loss of my dearest love can't. Death can't, life can't. Riots, wars, insanity, non-identity, hunger, neurosis, disease—none of these things, nor all of them heaped together can budge the fact that I am dearly loved, completely forgiven and forever free through Jesus Christ, your beloved son.

—RUTH CALKINS

It occurred to me one day that everything the devil does is designed for one purpose only: to draw us away from God's love. He does so not because he hates us, but because he hates God and will do anything to break His heart, and nothing breaks God's heart more than being separated from those He loves.

According to John Milton, the devil is the prowling Wolf,

Whom hunger drives to seek new haunt for prey,
Watching where Shepherds pen their flocks at eve
So climbs this grand thief into God's fold.

The Bible gives us a vivid picture of this enemy behind all enmity. Jesus described him as a *liar* and a *murderer* (John 8:44). His strategy is to deceive; his objective is to destroy. He is the source of all our doubts about God's goodness. He is the one behind the deceit that buffets us all day long—the messages that encourage us to find ourselves in something or someone more trustworthy than God; the subtle seductions to meet our needs our way rather than trust our Shepherd's wise provision. The devil fills us with guilt over the past, denying God's unfailing forgiveness. He makes us anxious about the present, insinuating that God cannot provide. He exacerbates the final terror of death, ignoring our Lord's conquest over the tomb.

The marks of Satan's presence are anxiety, guilt, and fear—all based on the lie that God either will not or cannot do anything about our condition; that our sin, our suffering, our inadequacy, our destiny—all are beyond His control or beyond His care. Satan's subtle craft is to make us suspicious of God: "He is holding out on you," he whispers in our ears. That's the devil's fundamental deception.

He's behind the bitterness of some of our questions: Why must little children become drug-dependent in utero? Why are women battered, abused, and then abandoned—discarded like pieces of waste? What of the homosexual's lonely despair? Does it occur to God that it is hard for us to live with only His invisible presence; that sometimes we long for human arms to give us a hug? Is He aware that His silence deafens us to His Word; that it's hard to believe He's still speaking to us today? Can He possibly comprehend the awful pain of our loneliness?

Satan plagues us with these questions and uses them to push us away from God.

We ask, "If God is so loving and kind, why is this?"

Any view of justice seems to demand that life ought to be better than it is, especially for those of us who want God and who are responsive to His love. God should go soft on us and give us the good life. Things should get easier as we get along in years, grow closer to Him, and get more in touch with His heart. For some that certainty is an article of faith, but God doesn't back up that creed.

We suffer. Painful, frustrating, discouraging, depressing, and costly things keep happening to us. Sorrow upon sorrow is often our lot, and sometimes the hardest parts of the journey are yet further along. All of this may convince us that the world is a very unfair place and leave us with serious doubt as to whether or not God is good.

But one thing we have to say about God: At least He took His own medicine. He subjected Himself to all the indignities and indecencies the world inflicts on us.

> Whatever the game he is playing with his creation, he has kept his own rules. He can exact nothing from man that he has not exacted from himself. He has himself gone through the whole of human experience, from the trivial irritations of family life and

the cramping restrictions of hard work and lack of money to the worst horrors of pain and humiliation, defeat, despair, and death. When He was a man, He played the man. He was born in poverty and died in disgrace and thought it well worthwhile.

—DOROTHY SAYERS

We look at our Lord's life and death here on earth and listen to His words and we say, "Here is one who understands what I'm going through!" He has experienced all of life's bitterness and heartache. He knows how difficult it is to burn the bridges we're called to destroy; He understands our inertia and our soul's resistance to change. He understands the power of sensual attraction. He has felt the disdain of others; He has seen their smirks and amused smiles; He has experienced coldness and the inability of others to understand. He knows. He understands. We can approach Him "with confidence [boldness], so that we may receive mercy and find grace to help us in our time of need" (Hebrews 4:16).

Doubts come and go, but we need not be dismayed by them. Doubt is not at first a sign that our faith has failed but that it's being assailed. When

doubts come we should counter by reminding ourselves of their source and that what the devil says
about God is not true—Satan is a liar. Then we can
renew our minds and strengthen our hearts with
the truth that God is the God "who does not lie"
(Titus 1:2). He is Eternal Good, and He is working
for our good.

For our good . . .

Paul writes: "We know that in all things God
works for the good of those who love him, who
have been called according to his purpose. For those
God foreknew he also predestined to be conformed
to the likeness of his Son, that he might be the first-
born among many brothers" (Romans 8:28–29).

Life is "a tale told by an idiot, full of sound
and fury, signifying nothing," wrote William
Shakespeare in *Macbeth*. God, however, says that
every circumstance has purpose. All things are
working together for good.

Of course, not everything that comes our
way is good. There is nothing good about cancer,
aging, or permanent disability. Life is often hard,
but God inspires the harshest events, transform-
ing them into advantage, exploiting them for

good. The hard occurrences crack our facades and reveal the neediness inside. They loosen our grip on the outside world as we see that its goodness is but an illusion, and then they draw our hearts inward to God's love. They center us on Him and conform us to His gracious will, for we have entered into this world for this purpose: "I have come to do your will, O God" (Hebrews 10:7). God uses every difficulty and complication to draw us to Himself and to conform us to His will. When it comes to that "good," any old circumstance will do.

> When God wants to drill a man
>   And thrill a man
>   And skill a man
> When God wants to mold a man
>   To play the noblest part;
> When he yearns with all his heart
>   To create a being so bold
> That all the world will be amazed,
>   watch his methods, watch his ways!
> How he relentlessly perfects
>   Whom he royally elects!
> How we're hammered and hurt
>   And with mighty blows converted

Into trial shapes of clay
Which only God understands;
While our tortured heart is crying
And we lift beseeching hands!
How God bends, but never breaks
When his good he undertakes;
How he uses whom he chooses
And with every purpose fuses us;
By every act induces us
To try his splendor out—
God knows what he's about!

—UNKNOWN

The severity of God is kinder than the kindness of man. As David put it, "Let us fall into the hands of the LORD, for his mercy is great; but do not let me fall into the hands of men" (2 Samuel 24:14). There is a love deeper than the love of those who seek only ease for those they love.

The nearness of God is our good . . .

One of David's fellow poets struggled valiantly with the goodness of God. "God is good to Israel, to those who are pure in heart," said Asaph rather lamely (Psalm 73:1). But the truth did not ring true. There was too much wrong with his world. He struggled intensely with his own pain and that of his neighbors. He couldn't understand why those who were pure in heart should have to suffer at all.

He was about to lose his grip on God: "But as for me, my feet had almost slipped; I had nearly lost my foothold. For I envied the arrogant when I saw the prosperity of the wicked" (73:2–3).

The "arrogant" are those who make no room in their lives for God. They give themselves all the credit; they never say thanks! They have a mindset like Toad Tarkington, one of writer Stephen Koontz's characters, who boasts, "Humble is for those who can't. I *can*."

The poet Asaph warmed to his task:

They [the arrogant] have no struggles;
    their bodies are healthy and strong.
They are free from the burdens common
    to man;
    they are not plagued by human ills.
Therefore pride is their necklace;
    they clothe themselves with violence.
From their callous hearts comes iniquity;
    the evil conceits of their minds know
        no limits.

They scoff, and speak with malice;
    in their arrogance they threaten
        oppression.
Their mouths lay claim to heaven,
    and their tongues take possession of
        the earth.
Therefore their [Hebrew: "his," i.e., God's]
        people turn to them
    and drink up waters in abundance.
They say, "How can God know?
    Does the Most High have knowledge?"
    [Does He know or care?]
This is what the wicked are like—
    always carefree, they increase in wealth.

—PSALM 73:4–12

The phrase "They have no struggles" might be translated "There are no pains in their death"—they die peacefully and painlessly. In contrast to the psalmist, who is plagued all day long (73:14), they are not plagued by human ills. They wear their pride boldly. Others observe their prosperity and "drink up waters in abundance." Using our idiom, they "drink it in," and it prejudices them against God.

Yet God, as the psalmist observed, continues to put up with human arrogance. He not only endures pride, He continues to provide the proud with good. "The rain rains on the just and on the unjust, but chiefly it rains on the just because the unjust steals his umbrella," laments an old adage.

The psalmist was dismayed: "Surely in vain have I kept my heart pure; in vain have I washed my hands in innocence," he lamented. "All day long I have been plagued; I have been punished every morning" (73:13–14).

The poet faced the full rigor of the problem: There's no payoff for knowing God. Why bother?

But then came a moment of truth: Asaph went into the place of revelation to hear what God had to say. There God disclosed an unknown or forgotten fact: This isn't all there is. There is more to life than the here and now. "When I tried to understand all this, it was oppressive to me till I entered the sanctuary of God; then I understood their final destiny [Hebrew: their *after*]" (Psalm 73:16–17). To use the poet's precise word, there is something *after*.

Although Asaph had little earthly good, he had God—forever! "I am always with you; you hold me by my right hand. You guide me with your counsel, and afterward you will take me into glory" (73:23–24).

This is the answer to all of Satan's lies: We may not have the good life—struggle, pain, disappointment, vexation, opposition, and loss may be our lot—but we have God, and God Himself is our good. "Happiness is neither outside nor inside us," Pascal said, "it is in God, both outside and inside us. . . . Our only true blessing is to be in him, and our sole ill to be cut off from him."

Life's disappointments show us how empty life is. Then, when the world's attractiveness begins to fade, we begin to move toward God as our good. As we come to Him again and again—listening to His Word, meditating on His thoughts, following Him in obedience, tasting of His goodness—He makes Himself increasingly known. We enter into intimacy with Him and come to love Him for Himself.

"The most fundamental need, duty, honor, and happiness of men is . . . adoration," said Friedrich von Hügel. In adoration we enjoy God for Himself. We long for the Giver rather than for His gifts. We ask nothing more than to be near Him and to be like Him. We want nothing but the hunger to give ourselves to Him. In adoration we learn why every other chase has left us breathless and restless, worn out and wanting for more.

And so, though it is hard to accept, we need nothing more than God's presence. Our toys and lesser joys can never satisfy; they are small delights. God *alone* is the answer to our deepest longings.

Once more we're confronted with unexpected simplicity: "The LORD is my shepherd, I shall not be in want." In this world or in the next, He is all we need.

So when I hear what God has to say I know the only thing left for me to do is to turn my energies toward Him, giving Him my full attention and my heart's devotion, asking Him every day to bring me to the place where I find Him more interesting than anyone I know, anything I do, any place I go, or anything I possess. It's a matter of centering myself on God. "Not consecration, but concentration," as Oswald Chambers said. Beyond salvation, beyond sanctification, beyond glorification lies the greatest joy of all: the joy of knowing God! (see Romans 5:1–11). It's what I was made for. If I do not *know* Him, my life is a failure.

> *Be thou my Vision, O Lord of my heart;*
> *Naught be all else to me, save that Thou art;*
> *Thou my best thought, by day or by night;*
> *Waking or sleeping, Thy presence my light.*

> —ELEANOR H. HULL, TRANSLATOR

All the days of my life . . .

God's goodness and love follow after us, cleaning up the messes we've left behind, undoing our wrongdoing (to the extent that it can be undone in this world), treating us as if it had never happened.

He follows us into our present, going behind and before, guiding us, leading us to pasture and still water, protecting us with His rod and staff, calling to the dispersed and gathering them in, carrying His lambs in His arms, leading us inexorably toward home.

Life is full of uncertainties, complexities, and complications. We have little power to change it or to mold it to our way. Every single day we face unknown, uncharted territory. There are no signs, landmarks, or milestones. We're left with Yogi Berra's ambiguity, "When you come to a fork in the road, take it."

What we need is a guide—someone who can give us wise counsel and bring discernment to our decisions.

Typically lost, we're always being escorted in the right direction; often perplexed, we're always on track. A. W. Tozer said boldly, "The man or woman who is wholly and joyously surrendered to

Christ cannot make a wrong choice." He means, of course, that our eternal destiny is not riding on our next decision. No choice that we make is final or ultimately fatal. We may take the oddest path through the wilderness, but we can be assured of this fact: Every day, whether we know it or not, we're being led along the path that leads us *home*.

We're inclined to think of God's help in terms of big decisions—where we will go to school, what career we will choose, where we will locate geographically, whom we will marry—when in fact life's biggest decision may be which way we turn when we leave our garage. Someone at the next intersection could run a red light and end or radically change our lives.

Life is hazardous—not merely a maze but a minefield! Who knows what eventualities lurk at the next crossroad? That uncertainty brings us to the place where all we can do is entrust ourselves to God and count on His goodness and love. "I am still confident of this," David said, "I will see the goodness of the LORD in the land of the living" (27:13). That confidence enables us to move bravely and optimistically into every day—as long as we know we are moving in the right direction.

"Which way do I want to go?" Alice asks the Cheshire Cat, "Would you tell me, please, which way I ought to go from here?" "That depends a good deal on where you want to get to," said the Cat. "I don't much care where—" says Alice. "Then it doesn't matter which way you go," replied the Cat.

—LEWIS CARROLL

Someone once pointed out to me that in terms of God there are only two options: we either say, "My will be done" or "Thy will be done." "Herein lies the healing of our confusion," Frank Buchman says, "make God the final authority! Not merely to say that with our lips, but with the discipline of the heart." Humility and docile acceptance of God's will are the essentials. We must give our wills to Him so He can make them His.

Those who do not want His way will miss it, but the one who is "firmly settled upon this, 'Whatever God wants, God helping me I will do it,' will not be left in doubt as to what God does wish him to do" (Alexander McLaren).

Jesus said, "The eye is the lamp of the body. If your eyes are good [focused on God], your whole body will be full of light. But if your eyes are bad [unfocused or trying to focus on more than one object], your whole body will be full of darkness. If then the light within you is darkness, how great is that darkness! (Matthew 6:22–23). If we want God and any other god we will always be in the dark, but if we fix our eyes on our Lord He will shed light on our way.

The wise man says, "Trust in the LORD with all your heart and lean not on your own understanding; in all your ways acknowledge him, and he will direct your paths (Proverbs 3:5–6). The question is always this: Do we want God's way? If so, He will direct our paths. The main thing is to want Him in all that we do and to entrust ourselves to His goodness every day—present ourselves before His face in humble submission—and leave the consequences to Him.

God's Word . . .

God has given His Word as our guide. As we read it He whispers His secrets into our ears; He "confides in those who fear him" (Psalm 25:14).

As we fill our minds with His thoughts we learn to discern good and evil; we learn to distinguish between the worthless and the worthwhile, the admirable and the ignoble. His Word enables us to make our way through life and to avoid the land mines. It gives us practical wisdom, it makes us street smart. We do well to saturate our minds with this erudition.

> We need minds so soaked with the content of Scripture, so imbued with biblical outlooks and principles, so sensitive to the Holy Spirit's prompting that we will know instinctively the upright step to take in any circumstances, small or great. Therefore the most important use of Scripture in relation to guidance is that through the study of it you may become acquainted with the ways and thoughts of God.
>
> —JOHN WHITE

Once, when Jesus was on His way to Jerusalem, His disciples took exception to His course: "Don't you know," they said, "they're planning to kill you there?" Their implication was that Jesus' judgment was flawed.

Jesus answered them with a question: "Are there not twelve hours of daylight? A man who walks by day will not stumble, for he sees by this world's light. It is when he walks by night that he stumbles, for he has no light" (John 11:9). His point was simply this: If God's Word is a lamp to our feet we will not wander too far from His way. We know in part and will surely err from time to time, but we will not make any ruinous mistakes— nothing that will impair the ultimate good of knowing God and enjoying Him.

The small stuff . . .

But what of the morally neutral decisions, the so-called small stuff of life: what we will eat or drink and what we will wear? We have little ground for uneasiness here. Unknown to us, God's compelling hand is behind every decision we make and everything we do. He cares about the bits and pieces of our days, and He arranged everything to suit Himself.

Our path is His business not ours. Our business is to trust Him with all our hearts and to refuse to rely on our own understanding. Certainly we must plan and prepare, but we must hold our schemes and dreams loosely, giving God the right to revise them or replace them without our approval or knowledge, permitting Him to advise us, correct us, inspire us, and prompt us, knowing that His compelling hand is directing everything we do.

Trusting Him to lead us means that we'll often be over our heads and out of control, living with uncertainty, giving up the security of our own plans, existing in a world where our confidence in God's goodness and love is the only sure thing.

Henri Nouwen writes, "The movement from illusion [the illusion that we are in control] to dependence is hard to make since it leads us from false certainties to true uncertainties, from an easy support system to a risky surrender, and from many 'safe' gods to the God whose love has no limits."

How true this is! To depend solely on God takes a special kind of humility on our part that admits that we cannot control the circumstances of our lives, that we do not have the answers to the hard questions of our existence, and that we are powerless to effect any eternal results. All we can do is trust our Shepherd's wisdom and love, and follow Him wherever He leads. But if we follow Him He will quietly, unobtrusively, direct our paths.

But we say, "How will I know what to do?"

I cannot tell you how. All I know is that when the time comes to know, we know. "He will help you," George MacDonald assures us, "Do not fear the 'how.'"

If we're uncertain, we should not hurry to decide what to do. We should rather wait—wait before God in silence and faith. He will speak; He is more willing to speak than we are to listen. He is, in fact, already speaking. It's only necessary to listen.

And so, as we make our way through life, we pray, as David prayed, "Show me your ways, O LORD, teach me your paths; guide me in your truth and teach me, for you are God my Savior, and my hope is in you all day long" (Psalm 25:4–5).

> *He's helping now—this moment,*
> *   Though I may not see it or hear,*
> *Perhaps by a friend far distant,*
> *   Perhaps by a stranger near,*
> *Perhaps by a spoken message,*
> *   Perhaps by the printed word;*
> *In ways that I know and know not*
> *   I have the help of the Lord.*
>
> *He's keeping me now—this moment,*
> *   However I need it most,*
> *Perhaps by a single angel,*
> *   Perhaps by a mighty host,*

Perhaps by the chain that frets me,
Or the walls that shut me in;
In ways that I know or know not
He keeps me from harm and sin.

He's guiding me now—this moment,
In pathways easy or hard,
Perhaps by a door wide open,
Perhaps by a door fast barred,
Perhaps by a joy withholden,
Perhaps by a gladness given;
In ways that I know and know not,
He's leading me up to heaven.

He's using me now—this moment,
And whether I go or stand,
Perhaps by a plan accomplished,
Perhaps when he stays my hand,
Perhaps by a word in season,
Perhaps by a silent prayer;
In ways that I know and know not,
His labor of love I share.

—ANNIE JOHNSON FLINT

I will dwell in the house of the LORD forever . . .

Is any promise sweeter in all our Father's Word?
"I will dwell forever in the house of the Lord."

—ANNIE JOHNSON FLINT

There's a natural watershed in our lives. We reach the top, stand for a moment, and then we're over the hill. Everything is downhill from that moment on. But no matter; we're headed for home.

> *Home from those wayward wanderings,*
> *Home from that cold foreign clime,*
> *Home, to the arms of "Our Father,"*
> *Where I am all His and He's mine.*
>
> —OSWALD CHAMBERS

Home—that's where my heart is.

"I have come home at last!" shouted C. S. Lewis's heaven-struck unicorn as he stamped his right fore-hoof on the ground. "I have come home at last! This is my real country! I belong here. This is the land I have been looking for all my life, though I never knew it till now. The reason why we loved the old Narnia is that it sometimes looked a little like this."

It's not that heaven is somewhat like home. It *is* home. Our earthly homes are mere signs or reflections—primitive symbols of warmth, love, togetherness, and familiarity. The ultimate reality is our Father's house—where there is a father who never dies, who makes a home for the lonely, who treats us like family; where real love awaits us; where we're included—"taken in."

We hear about Odysseus, the Flying Dutchman, Frodo, and E.T., and we too want to go home—to that place where everything is impervious to change, where God will wipe every tear from our eyes, where we can cease "to break our wings against the faultiness of things," where everyone has a friend, where love will never end, where everything finally works out for good.

Everything goes wrong here; nothing will go wrong there. Nothing will be lost; nothing will be missing; nothing will fall apart or go down the drain. Heaven is God's answer to Murphy's Law.

Not all our hurts can be healed in this life. There are wounds we will bear all our lives, but, as a friend once said to me, "If you hold your wounds up to the sunlight of God's love they will never fester and in heaven they will be healed." Some harm awaits heaven's cure. That's where that "great bleeding wound from which all of us suffer will be eternally healed" (C. S. Lewis).

In this life we're delivered from shame, guilt, and fear by God's forgiving love; there is substantial improvement, but there's no complete healing. We were born with broken hearts, and some sense of that brokenness will be with us throughout our days on earth. We'll never quite be whole. There will always be some measure of inner pain that will coexist with our joy and peace, some vague longing—homesickness—that will linger until we get home. We are satisfied here, but never quite content.

One of these days we'll go home and then everything will be complete. Think of a place where there is no sin, no sorrow, no quarrels, no threats, no abandonment, no insecurity, no struggling with sagging self-worth. Heaven is where everything that makes us sad will be banished. We will be delivered from everything that has defiled or disrupted our lives.

It's disturbing to look ahead and see the same impossible road stretching out in front of us, going on indefinitely. We're driven to despair or rebellion when we think there's no point to our misery and no end to it. That's why we find comfort in the realization that it will *not* go on forever. One day, everything that God has been doing will be done. He will come for us and we will go home.

It may surprise you to know that David knew that much about heaven. Most folks who read the Old Testament never think to look for heaven there, but it occurs—in symbol and song, in metaphor and type. Ancient people took to analogy much better than we. They drew pictures: green pastures, Elysian fields, light. One of the most convincing images is that of God Himself taking us in.

The thought occurs in the story of Enoch, who walked with God for three hundred years and "then he was no more, because God took him away" (Genesis 5:24). Enoch and God took a walk one day and got too far from home. The old patriarch was too weary to walk all the way back so God took him.

One of Israel's singers saw himself and others as "destined for the grave," but as he goes on to say, "God will redeem my life from the grave; he will surely take me to himself" (Psalm 49:14–15).

And then there's the poet who learned God's presence from his peril: "I am always with you," he concluded. For now, "you hold me by my right hand. You guide me with your counsel, and afterward you will take me into glory" (Psalm 73:23–24).

Taken in. I like that way of looking at my death. It reminds me of something Jesus said: "I am going . . . to prepare a place for you. And if I go and prepare a place for you, I will come back and take you to be with me that you also may be where I am" (John 14:2–3).

That's the fundamental revelation of heaven in both Testaments: being taken in, welcomed, received, embraced, included. Death for God's children is not bitter frustration, but mere transition into a larger and permanent love—a love undisturbed by time, unmenaced by evil, unbroken by fear, unclouded by doubt.

All God's idylls end favorably; all God's children live happily forever after. That's the most cherished article of my creed.

> Never again will they hunger;
>   never again will they thirst.
> The sun will not beat upon them,
>   nor any scorching heat.
> For the Lamb at the center of the throne
>   will be their shepherd;
>   he will lead them to springs of living water.
> And God will wipe away
>   every tear from their eyes.

—REVELATION 7:16–17

NOTE TO THE READER

The publisher invites you to share your response to the message of this book by writing Discovery House Publishers, Box 3566, Grand Rapids, MI 49501, USA. For information about other Discovery House books, music, or videos, contact us at the same address or call 1-800-653-8333. Find us on the Internet at http://www.dhp.org/ or send e-mail to books@dhp.org.